Chris L. Kleinke is Assistant Professor of Psychology at Wheaton College in Norton, Massachusetts. He has previously taught at Claremont Men's College and served as research consultant for the Riverside, California, Unified School District. Dr. Kleinke's research in first impressions and nonverbal communication has been published in leading professional journals.

Chris L. Kleinke

FIRST IMPRESSIONS

The Psychology
Of Encountering Others

A SPECTRUM BOOK

PRENTICE-HALL, INC., Englewood Cliffs, New Jersey

Library of Congress Cataloging in Publication Data

KLEINKE, CHRIS L
  First impressions.

  (A Spectrum Book)
  Includes bibliographical references and index.
  1. Nonverbal communication. I. Title.
BF637.C45K54   158'.2   75-2074
  ISBN 0-13-318436-6
  ISBN 0-13-318428-5 pbk.

© 1975 by PRENTICE-HALL, INC.
ENGLEWOOD CLIFFS, NEW JERSEY

A SPECTRUM BOOK

10 9 8 7 6 5 4

Printed in the United States of America

PRENTICE-HALL INTERNATIONAL, INC. *(London)*
PRENTICE-HALL OF AUSTRALIA PTY., LTD. *(Sydney)*
PRENTICE-HALL OF CANADA, LTD. *(Toronto)*
PRENTICE-HALL OF INDIA PRIVATE LIMITED *(New Delhi)*
PRENTICE-HALL OF JAPAN, INC. *(Tokyo)*

To Meem-Meem, Carl La Fong, and Max

Contents

Preface

A couple meeting for the first time, a man or woman interviewing for a job, and a salesperson all share the desire to make a favorable first impression. Each of us has been curious at one time or another as to why it is that we immediately like some people at first meeting, immediately dislike other people at first meeting, and are indifferent toward still other people when we first meet them. Novelists, poets, and song writers have, for centuries, provided us with extensive insights from their observations about the ways people come to perceive one another. Social scientists have studied how people form first impressions by using objective methods of research in measuring and controlling relevant variables. This book summarizes scientific studies about how people form first impressions. Some of the experiments may appear artificial. A few may strike you as humorous. Within these possible limitations, you will find that the information contained in this book is based not on intuition, but on controlled measurement. Some of this knowledge should be of interest to you. Certain aspects may even be of practical value. At the very least this material will, I hope, satisfy some of your curiosity about first impressions between people as they interact in their day-to-day lives.

Last line in oral report — I hope, I have satisfied some of your curiosity about first impressions.

I

Looks Aren't Everything,
But . . .

As the saying has it, beauty is only skin deep. Or, as another cliché asserts, "You can't judge a book by its cover." When we meet someone for the first time, however, we are often limited to skin-deep observations. For this reason, it is not surprising that outside appearance would constitute a large part of the information we use to form a first impression. Book publishers and record companies are well aware of this, judging from the efforts and expense they invest in designing covers that will be attractive to prospective buyers.

If you ask yourself how one can study the effects of physical attractiveness on impression formation it might occur to you that this would be difficult because different people have different tastes. What is beautiful to one person may not be beautiful to another. It is true that we may not agree exactly on which specific physical traits we prefer. Some people prefer blondes, other people prefer brunettes. Some of us are attracted to long hair on men or women, others are partial to men or women with short hair. Despite individual differences on specific aspects of physical appearance, however, there is an overall tendency for people to agree on who is attractive and who is not so attractive. Ellen Berscheid and Elaine Walster, social psychologists at the universities of Minnesota and Wisconsin, have done extensive research on the subject of physical attractiveness. In one article they summarize a number of studies showing that people agree quite closely when they are asked to rate photographs on a numerical scale of attractiveness.[1] There is also a much higher amount of agreement between males and females than you might expect. The tendency for people to judge attractiveness in a fairly consistent manner is learned at an early age. The development of attractiveness perception has been measured by asking children at various age levels to make ratings of photographs. Studies which have followed this procedure show that by the age of seven, children agree quite consistently with each other and with adults on how they judge the attractiveness of other children as well as other adults.[2,3]

The fact that people learn to agree from a young age about who is attractive and who is not attractive is important for our discussion here because it implies that certain general rules can be made about the effects of physical appearance on impression formation, at least for people within the same culture. How has physical attractiveness been studied? A common method, as you might guess, is to show people photographs of attractive and unattractive men and women and have them make ratings or judgments of one kind or another. Other studies have arranged for participants to be exposed to real people who vary in attractiveness.

ATTRACTIVENESS IN PHOTOGRAPHS

What You See Is What You Get. Although the use of photographs to study physical attractiveness is somewhat artificial, it does present the advantage of controlling other important factors which might affect people's first impressions, such as gestures, tone of voice, and facial expressions.

Arthur G. Miller conducted an experiment at Miami University in Ohio in which he asked male and female students to look at a photograph of someone their own age and make ratings of the person in the photograph on seventeen adjective dimensions. The photographs used in the study had previously been separated by judges into categories of high, medium, and low physical attractiveness. Students rated males and females in the photographs who were highly attractive as significantly more curious, complex, perceptive, confident, assertive, happy, active, amiable, candid, serious, pleasure-seeking, outspoken, and flexible than males and females in the photographs who were low in attractiveness.* In

---

* The term "significant" means that a statistical test has been applied to the results and has found them to be consistent and reliable, rather than a matter of chance. This definition will be used throughout the book.

addition, male students rated males and females who were highly attractive as significantly more careful and cooperative, compared with males and females who were low in physical attractiveness. Female students also saw highly attractive males and females as significantly more calm and academic than unattractive males and females. Miller's conclusion was that:

A consistent pattern emerges, that of the unattractive person being associated with the negative or undesirable pole of the adjective scales and the highly attractive person being judged significantly more positively.[4]

In another study by Miller in which students judged the same photographs it was found that highly attractive males and females were seen as having a large degree of inner control over their own behavior and as "masters of their own fate, as individuals who behave with a sense of purpose and out of their own volition." Unattractive males and females, on the other hand, were judged as having much less control over their own fate and as "coerced and generally influenced by others or by environmental conditions."[5]

A similar study was carried out at the University of Texas in which students were asked to look at a yearbook picture of another student whom they did not know and give an opinion about how much they liked the person in the picture and how much they would like to be paired with the person as a work partner. Both male and female students preferred males and females in the pictures who had been previously rated by judges as physically attractive.[6]

Students at the University of North Carolina were asked to rate an opposite-sex person in a yearbook photograph on the basis of how much they liked the person in the photograph and how much they would be willing to be involved with the person in a working, dating, or marriage relationship. The yearbook photographs had previously been divided by judges into categories of high, medium, and low physical attractiveness. Ratings of male students were affected by physical attractiveness to a somewhat greater degree than ratings of female students. Though physical attractiveness had more of an influence in dating choice than on liking, working, or marriage, both male and female students gave the highest preference in all categories to the highly attractive people in the photographs. Unattractive opposite-sex persons were given significantly lower preference on all four types of involvement.[7]

A very provocative study was conducted by Karen Dion and her colleagues. Men and women students at the University of Minnesota were asked to give their impressions of other students from whatever information they could gather in a photograph. The photographs used in the study were of high, medium, and low attractive men and women. The attractiveness of the males and females in the photographs had a significant influence on how they were judged by students on the following traits:

Social desirability of personality, occupational status, marital competence, social and professional happiness, and total happiness.

Highly attractive males and females were given the most favorable rating on every trait and unattractive males and females always received the most unfavorable rating. The only issue on which physical attractiveness did not make a difference was judgment of parental competence. High, average, and low attractive men and women in the photographs were rated equally on what kinds of parents they might be. Dion and her colleagues had felt that the participants in their study might have jealousy toward highly attractive members of their own sex and compensate for this by giving highly attractive same-sex persons relatively unfavorable ratings. This did not prove to be the case. Both men and women participants preferred highly attractive males in the photographs as well as highly attractive females in the photographs. What is beautiful is good.[8] Dion concluded her research report with a quote from Florence Monahan:

Even social workers accustomed to dealing with all types often find it difficult to think of a normal, pretty girl as being guilty of a crime. Most people, for some inexplicable reason, think of crime in terms of abnormality in appearance, and I must say that beautiful women are not often convicted.[9]

Male students at the University of Rochester were asked to evaluate an essay which they thought was written by a woman whose picture was attached. The pictures used in the study were of attractive or unattractive women and the essays were made up to be either very good or very poor. Overall, men rated the essays much more favorably if they thought they had been written by an attractive rather than by an unattractive woman. In addition, the poor essays attributed to attractive women were evaluated almost as positively as the good essays supposedly written by unattractive women. Beauty is talent! [10]

ATTRACTIVENESS AT AN EARLY AGE

We saw earlier that children learn to agree on who is attractive and who is unattractive at an early age. Do children also have preference for other children who are attractive rather than unattractive? Karen Dion and Ellen Berscheid attempted to answer this question by showing nursery-school children pictures of their classmates and asking them to make certain choices and ratings. The pictures of the children had been divided by adult judges into categories of high and low physical attractiveness. Adult judges were presumably used because of convenience, but we already know that the ratings of adults and children on attractiveness are very similar. When asked to choose which classmates they especially liked, both boys and girls picked out attractive boys significantly more often than unattractive boys. In the very youngest group of nursery-school children (about four to five and a half years), unattractive girls were more popular than attractive girls. It is possible that unattractive girls learn certain compensatory social behaviors to win approval at a young age which are later overshadowed by the increased importance of physical appearance. Older nursery-school children (five and a half to seven years) liked attractive girls significantly more often than they liked unattractive girls. When asked to point out who they thought was aggressive and fought or shouted a lot, both boys and girls chose unattractive boys significantly more often than attractive boys. When asked who was afraid of a lot of things both boys and girls chose unattractive girls significantly more often than they chose attractive girls. The nursery-school children also judged that unattractive boys and girls were significantly more "scary" and significantly more dependent than attractive boys and girls.[11] A similar tendency for college students to see unattractive persons as more dependent than attractive persons was discussed earlier. Dion and Berscheid feel that the disposition for children to prefer peers who are attractive rather than unattractive has a circular effect. If unattractive children are perceived differently from attractive children, they are treated differently. And if unattractive children are treated differently, they begin to act differently. There is evidence that adults give more favorable treatment to children who are attractive than they give to children who are unattractive.

Preferential Treatment by Adults. Teachers from 400 elementary schools were each provided with a summary record and photograph of a fifth-grade student. The records for all students were the same and arranged to appear above average. The photographs were varied so that some of the teachers judged students who were attractive and some of the teachers judged students who were unattractive. Results showed that both male and female teachers judged that attractive boys and girls had significantly higher IQs, significantly better social relationships with classmates, significantly higher educational potential, and parents with significantly better attitudes toward school as compared with boys and girls who were low in attractiveness. The fact that teachers can look at identical records of students and interpret them favorably if the student is attractive and unfavorably if the student is unattractive gives reason for concern.[12]

Female university students were given a description of a misbehavior that had been committed by a seven-year-old boy or girl, along with the child's photograph. The students were asked to offer their opinions about the child, who was either attractive or unattractive, on a number of issues. When the misbehavior which the boys and girls had supposedly committed was severe, such as throwing a hard snowball at another child and cutting his head, the female students were much more lenient when the boys and girls were attractive. A misbehavior committed by an attractive child tended to be attributed to the child's having had a bad day. The following comment was typical:

> She appears to be a perfectly charming little girl, well mannered, basically unselfish. It seems that she can adapt well among children her age and make a good impression . . . she plays well with everyone, but like anyone else, a bad day can occur. Her cruelty . . . need not be taken too seriously.[13]

When an unattractive child committed the same undesirable behavior he or she was much more likely to be seen as generally bad, such as in the following example:

> I think the child would be quite bratty and would be a problem to teachers . . . she would probably try to pick a fight with other children her own age . . . she would be a brat at home . . . all in all, she would be a real problem.[14]

Unattractive children were perceived by the female students as being significantly more dishonest and unpleasant than attractive children, even though they had committed the same act. A misbehavior engaged in by an unattractive child was rated as significantly more undesirable than the same misbehavior performed by an attractive child. Female students did not differ in the severity of punishment they recommended for attractive and unattractive children. It is likely, though, that people might differ in other ways in how they treat misbehaviors of attractive versus unattractive children. It was felt that the use of female university students as judges in this study was appropriate because of the strong socializing influence that women of this age have on children, both in school and in the home.[15]

ATTRACTIVENESS IN BLIND DATES

What is the first thing that people ask when somebody offers to set them up with a blind date? "What does he or she look like?" Right?

The Computer Dance. In the mid-1960's a dance was organized for freshmen students at the University of Minnesota where students could purchase tickets for a dollar and be matched (supposedly by computer) with a date for the evening. When students came to the student union to buy their tickets they were secretly rated on how physically attractive they were by four sophomores who were working for the experiment. The men and women who bought tickets were matched randomly as dates with one limitation: a man was never paired with a date taller than he was. The several hundred couples were ushered into various rooms during the intermission to make ratings of each other on a questionnaire. The results of the study, by this time, will not surprise you. When asked how much they liked their date and whether they would like to date the same person again, both men and women gave significantly more preference to dates who had previously been rated by the experimenters as physically attractive. Scores from a wide variety of personality tests which had been obtained from the University's testing service did not relate to how much the men and women were preferred as dates. A date's physical attractiveness was somewhat more important to men than it was to women, but both men and women showed a clear tendency to use physical attractiveness as the main basis on which they evaluated their dates. It is interesting that the manner in which participants evaluated their dates had no relationship to how their dates evaluated them. This was probably due to the fact that the couples did not know each other well and could not judge accurately how their dates really felt about them.[16]

A similar dance organized at Penn State University a few years later found essentially the same results. Participants were much more likely to want to date their partners again if the partners were physically attractive. When asked to specify other people at the dance whom they would like to date, both male and female participants overwhelmingly chose persons who were highly attractive.[17]

Students who participated in a computer dance at Purdue University stated that physical attractiveness and "personality" were the most important factors in deciding whether they liked their dates and would like to go out with them in the future.[18]

The Coke Date. A slightly different kind of dating study was carried out at the University of Texas. Students were paired with a date who was either similar or dissimilar to them on a number of attitudes and opinions which had been measured earlier. When the participants arrived at the experiment and met their dates they were given fifty cents and sent to the student union to get to know each other for a half hour. The couples then returned to rate each other on a questionnaire. Both males and females had greater preference for dates who had earlier been determined to be similar to them and to dates who were physically attractive. Participants who thought their dates were physically attractive were more likely to rate them as personally and sexually attractive and as desirable dating or marriage partners than participants who saw their dates as unattractive. When contacted two or three months after the experiment, participants with similar and physically attractive dates showed the greatest likelihood of remembering their date's name, of having talked with their date in the meantime, and of expressing the desire to date again in the future.[19]

ATTRACTIVENESS IN INTERACTIONS

Another method for studying physical attractiveness has been to compare the reactions of men to a woman who has been made up to look either pretty or ugly. The use of the same woman as both an attractive and unattractive stimulus is experimentally advantageous because factors such as tone of voice, posture, and gestures are fairly well controlled.

In one study of the effects of attractiveness on opinion change it was found that an attractive female student could increase her influence in changing the opinions of male students if she openly stated her desire to influence them before she gave her argument. This tactic of openness was not successful for the female when she was unattractive. When males were asked to rate the female they stated that she was significantly more charming, fashionable, neat, romantic, affectionate, likable, and significantly less unpleasant, annoying, and emotional when she was attractive than when she was unattractive.[20]

In another experiment it was arranged that male students would receive either a positive or negative evaluation from a female who was made up to be attractive or unattractive. As you would expect, the males liked the evaluator better when she was attractive and when her evaluations were positive. In addition, it turned out that it was a lot more important to the men how they were evaluated by the attractive female.

When they were being evaluated by the unattractive female the men didn't care so much whether her evaluations were positive or negative.[21]

The effects of physical attractiveness on impression formation are contagious. A study was conducted in which men were introduced while accompanied by either an attractive or unattractive girl friend. The men were later rated significantly more favorably in terms of their overall character and how likable they were if the woman with whom they had been associated was attractive. In addition, the men themselves *expected* to be viewed more positively when they were associated with an attractive rather than an unattractive woman.[22]

WHAT MAKES PEOPLE PHYSICALLY ATTRACTIVE?

The studies of physical attractiveness that we have considered so far compared people who were judged to be attractive with other people who were judged unattractive. No attempt has been made up to this point to specify exactly which features or traits differentiate between attractive and unattractive people. You can well imagine that it is easier for people to agree generally about who is attractive and who is unattractive than it is for people to agree on which specific attributes they prefer in which specific person. We have all had experiences in which we felt that someone was particularly attractive (or unattractive), but found it difficult to state in words exactly why we felt the way we did. Some investigators have tried to measure reactions to certain traits or features about people and find out which ones might be preferred more than others.

Bad Breath, Glasses, Lipstick, and Beards. It might be interesting to look first at a few historical studies whose results may or may not still apply today.

In 1921 Perrin asked men and women at the University of Texas to give descriptions of fellow students who had previously been judged as either attractive or unattractive. The traits most often associated with attractive females were:

clean hair, clean teeth, care to avoid unpleasant breath, care in coughing, care of eyes, hair in prevalent fashion, aristocratic bearing, and general care of body.

Unattractive females were identified by:

shape of chin, proportions of bust, shoulders and hips, expressions of eyes and mouth, lack of care of hair, lack of taste and neatness in dress, absence of aristocratic bearing, and poor physical poise.

Attractive males were described as avoiding unpleasant breath and taking care of their body. Unattractive males were judged according to displeasing shape of eyes, ears, mouth, and lips, lack of care of hands and nails, general lack of care of body, and absence of aristocratic bearing. Two conclusions reached in this study were that men and women have pretty much the same standards for beauty in both sexes and that the traits associated with physical attractiveness have more to do with how a person acts than with his or her specific features.[23]

In 1944 another group of investigators asked students to judge men and women in photographs or in real life. Half of the time the people being judged wore glasses and half of the time they did not. Results showed that both in photographs and real life, men and women with glasses were judged as significantly more intelligent and industrious than men and women without glasses. There were no consistent differences between people with and without glasses in judgments of honesty, kindness, dependability, and sense of humor.[24]

In a 1952 study men students interviewed college women for ten minutes and then gave their impressions of the women on a rating form. Half of the time women wore lipstick and half of the time they did not. Women wearing lipstick were rated as more frivolous, placid, introspective, and conscientious than women without lipstick.[25]

More recently, a number of undergraduates were questioned about their feeling toward beardedness. The measures taken were somewhat loose, but showed a tendency for men to perceive bearded men as independent and extroverted. Women gave an indication of perceiving men with beards as masculine, sophisticated, and mature.[26]

In a more controlled study, eight men between twenty-two and twenty-five years of age were paid ten dollars to shave off their beards. The shaving was done by a barber and photographs were taken of the men at four stages: full beard, goatee, moustache, clean-shaven. When college students were asked to give their impressions of the men in the photographs they showed a consistent tendency to give more favorable ratings to men with the most facial hair. Men with full beards were evaluated as significantly more masculine, mature, good-looking, dominant, self-confident, courageous, liberal, nonconformist, and industrious than clean-shaven men. Men with moustaches and goatees fell in between.

It isn't certain whether people other than college students would be so favorable toward men with beards, but it was suggested by the author of the study that inside many men "there is a beard screaming to be let out." [27]

"Clothes Make the Man." Several investigators have produced support for this old adage. In one study it was found that the evaluation of men in photographs could be altered by changing their dress.[28] Another researcher had students rate color drawings of various types of clothing to demonstrate that clothes, and presumably the people wearing them, can be identified according to political and ideological stereotypes.[29]

In an experiment conducted in Austin, Texas, it was arranged that a thirty-one-year-old male "model" would come to an intersection in the presence of other pedestrians and either obey or violate the pedestrian crossing signal. When the model was well dressed in a coat and tie, significantly more people would follow his example in disobeying the "wait" signal than when the model was poorly dressed in work clothes.[30]

People using phone booths in Grand Central Station and Kennedy Airport in New York City were approached by a male or female college student with the following request: "Excuse me, Sir (Miss), I think I might have left a dime in this phone booth a few minutes ago. Did you find it?" The college students had secretly placed a dime in the phone booth a few minutes before and wanted to see if the person confronted would return the dime. Half of the time the college men wore suits and ties and the college women wore neat dresses and a dress coat. During the other times the men wore work clothes and the women wore skirts and blouses which were generally unkempt in appearance. Significantly more people returned the dime when they were approached by the well-dressed college students.[31]

Two college psychology teachers each came to their first classes wearing the black suit and Roman collar of the Catholic priest. For another class the same teachers wore coats and ties. When asked to give their first impressions of the teachers, the classes to which they had come in priestly dress rated them as significantly more moral, reputable, unusual, and also as more withdrawn, than the classes to which they had come in regular dress. Nine weeks later one of the teachers was rated again. The class to which he had worn priestly dress rated him significantly more introverted, solitary, unscientific, self-contained, and discouraging than the class where he wore a coat and tie. The effect of clothing on impressions did not disappear over time. It would be interesting to know whether the stereotype of dress had remained in the students' minds for nine weeks or whether the teacher actually behaved differently when he was dressed in different ways.[32]

High-school students were photographed in four different kinds of dress: high-school uniform, casual clothes, working clothes, and evening clothes. The rating descriptions which college students gave to the people in the pictures depended significantly on their dress. The male and female high-school students tended to be rated as pleasant when they were in evening dress, youthful when they had on high-school uniforms, relaxed and happy in casual dress, active when they wore work clothes (and interesting when dressed in either evening or casual clothes.)[33]

Beauty Hint: Lose Weight.   Every day in the newspaper there are ads for weight reduction and countless programs for improving every conceivable aspect of one's physical appearance. None of you need to be reminded that obesity is a stigma in American society. Other kinds of physical disabilities that people suffer are generally attributed to misfortune and elicit a certain amount of sympathy and understanding. Obesity, on the other hand, is most often associated with laziness or lack of will power. When obese people are discriminated against there is the feeling that they deserve it because they could lose weight if they wanted to. This aversion to obesity is held by people in our culture of all ages.

Ten- and eleven-year-old children were shown drawings of a normal child, a child with crutches and brace on one leg, a child sitting in a wheel chair, a child with the left hand missing, a child with facial disfigurement, and an obese child. When asked to rank the drawings in order of preference the children consistently rated the obese child as the least liked. The tendency to give the lowest preference to the obese child was consistent for male and female children from a wide range of ethnic and social backgrounds.[34] A group of professional adults were given the same test and also rated the obese child as being least desirable.[35]

Adults were asked to look at silhouette drawings or read descriptions of men having one of three body builds: (a) soft, fat, round; (b) muscular, athletic; (c) tall, thin, fragile. The adults felt that men with the three different body builds were characterized by the following traits:[36, 37]

(a) *soft, fat, round*—fat, old, short, old-fashioned, physically weak, ugly, talkative, warmhearted, sympathetic, good-natured, agreeable, dependent on others, trusting, greedy for affection, oriented toward people, loving physical comfort, loving eating.

(b) *muscular, athletic*—strong, masculine, good-looking, adventurous, tall, self-reliant, energetic, youthful, competitive, liking exercise, bold.

(c) *tall, thin, fragile*—thin, young, ambitious, tall, suspicious, tense, nervous, stubborn, difficult, pessimistic, quiet, sensitive to pain, liking privacy, inhibited, secretive.

When boys six to ten years old were asked to assign adjectives of various traits to silhouettes representing three types of body build they showed clear preference for the muscular, athletic build. A person with a round, fat body build was characterized by the boys as cheating, argumentative, being teased a lot, forgetful, lazy, unhealthy, lying, sloppy, naughty, ugly, mean, dumb, and dirty. One with a very thin body build was evaluated as being weak, quiet, lonely, sneaky, afraid, and sad.[38]

Five- and six-year-old children who looked at photographs (with the head covered) of chubby, average, or thin children their own age expressed a consistent aversion to the chubby child.[39] Males ranging in age from ten to twenty years gave pictures of men with muscular body builds positive ratings and pictures of fat or very thin men negative ratings. The fat men were characterized as being the poorest athletes, drinking and eating the most, having few friends, being unaggressive, enduring pain the least, and being the most likely to have a nervous breakdown.[40]

A survey taken in New England found that more nonobese high school graduates went on to college than high school graduates who were obese. When these results were published in *The New York Times*, they appeared under the headline[41]:

COLLEGE ADMISSION HINT: LOSE WEIGHT

Male students who were interviewed at Rutgers University stated that a main reason they did not like to be seen with a heavy girl was fear of ridicule.[42] Female college students who were questioned about their ideal figure specified that they would prefer to weigh less and to have smaller waists and hips and larger busts.[43]

Elevator Shoes, Anyone? One factor which has a far-reaching influence on how people are perceived, at least in American society, is height. From 1900 to 1968 the man elected U.S. president was always the taller of the two candidates (Richard Nixon was slightly shorter than George McGovern).

In a survey of University of Pittsburgh graduates it was found that men who were taller (six feet two inches and over) received average starting salaries 12.4 percent higher than men who were shorter (under six feet).[44] Another survey asked 140 corporate recruiters to choose between two job applicants after reading their applications. It was arranged that the hypothetical applicants had exactly the same qualifications. The only difference was that one was listed as six feet one inch and the other as five feet five inches. The short man was favored by only 1 percent of the recruiters. Seventy-two percent of the recruiters said they would rather hire the tall man and 27 percent had no preference.[45]

An interesting experiment was conducted in which a visitor was introduced to five similar groups of college students. In each group the visitor was given a different status, such as student, demonstrator, lecturer, senior lecturer, or full professor. Later, the students were asked to estimate the visitor's height, supposedly for use in a statistics exercise. It turned out clearly that the visitor was perceived by students as taller when his status was high and shorter when his status was low.[46] A similar study had nursing students estimate the heights of the assistant director of their school, their instructor, their class president, and a specified fellow student. The heights of the staff figures were overestimated, with the height of the assistant director being overestimated the most. The heights of the two students were underestimated, with the height of the fellow student being reduced the most.[47]

A sample of California voters during the 1960 Kennedy-Nixon election evaluated whichever candidate they had selected as being the taller of the two.[48] People who expressed liking for Lyndon Johnson when he was in office estimated him as being taller than did people who disliked him.[49] People who were shown slides of members of different ethnic groups who were of equal height estimated the members of ethnic groups they preferred as being taller than members of ethnic groups they did not favor.[50]

We are all aware of the unwritten rule that the male member of a couple must not be shorter than the female. Studies of adolescents have shown that boys tend more to worry about being short and girls worry most often about being tall.[51]

LOOKS ARE IMPORTANT

Elliot Aronson, a well-known social psychologist, feels that physical attractiveness has been neglected as an area of study because social scientists are democratic and want to believe that beautiful and ugly people are equal. By avoiding the study of physical attractiveness, social scientists can escape from the possibility that looks really are important in how a person is judged.[52]

People from a wide variety of populations consistently underemphasize the importance of attractiveness when they are asked which traits are important to them in a potential dating or marriage partner.[53] The extensive research showing that physical appearance *is* an important factor in first impressions has led some investigators to conclude that people "are either not fully aware or not fully honest about how important physical attractiveness really is to them." [54] Looks do count. In fact, at least one psychologist has argued that plastic surgery can be a valuable alternative or addition to psychotherapy in the improvement of one's self concept, behavior, and the treatment he or she receives from others:

> For example, if an unattractive girl requests psychotherapy because she feels lonely and rejected and cannot find a husband, it might be more advantageous in terms of time and expense to consider plastic surgery. Rather than have the girl spend months or years in expensive therapy trying to discover her intrapsychic difficulties, it might be better to help her integrate and adjust to the changes which might result from plastic surgery.[55]

Inmates from the New York City jail system were given cosmetic surgery to correct disfigurements ranging from knife and burn scars to lop-ears and tattoos. Compared with a similar group of prisoners who did not receive cosmetic surgery, the "beautified" prisoners who were nonaddicts had a significantly lower rate of recidivism. The plastic surgery did not reduce the recidivism of addicts. It was concluded from these results that although the cost of plastic surgery in the rehabilitation of adult offenders is relatively high, it "can be considered negligible if the offender is helped to remain out of prison for even one year." [56]

IS THERE ANY HOPE FOR THE REST OF US?

Looks are important, but looks aren't everything. Even though attractive people are viewed more favorably on first impression than unattractive people, they are not necessarily happier or better adjusted. In addition, attractiveness has its primary influence in situations of first meeting. In sustained interactions we become judged more on the basis of who we are and what we do rather than how we look.

Are Beautiful People Better Adjusted? Although there are no specific data, I think it would be safe to say that physical attractiveness has had little bearing on the kinds of contributions and achievements people have been able to make in the history of the world. We might expect that physically attractive people would be happier because of the favorable evaluation and treatment they receive. People who are satisfied with their physical appearance do seem to feel better about other parts of themselves.[57] Berscheid and Walster make the very important point, however, that the degree to which we are satisfied with our physical appearance has a lot to do with the standards we set for ourselves.[58] We have to accept not being the most beautiful person in the world. Happiness is very subjective and depends more on our attitudes than our specific appearance. It is difficult, therefore, to conceive of objectively measuring the comparative happiness of attractive and unattractive people. One thing that can be said is that attractive children and beautiful women who have lost their good looks through maturation probably suffer the most because they no longer receive the attention that they have become used to.

Beauty Is as Beauty Does. Our society has increasingly become oriented toward one-time social contacts. Jobs such as stewardess and receptionist make use of the power of beauty on first impressions. Berscheid and Walster suggest that attractive people might even tend to prefer one-time to long-time interpersonal contacts because of their advantage at first meetings.[59] Yet, in the relationships which are most important to us, the way we act ends up being more important than how we look. Perrin summarized his finding in 1921 that behaviors have more to do with judgments of attractiveness than specific traits, with the conclusion that "Beauty is as beauty does." [60] Research has shown that as we get to know a person better we rely less and less on his or her physical appearance for our evaluations.[61,62]

Beauty *is* only skin deep. It is important for first impressions, but not so important for interactions over time.

NOTES

1 E. BERSCHEID and E. WALSTER, "Physical Attractiveness," in L. Berkowitz (Ed.), *Advances in Experimental Social Psychology*, Vol. 7 (New York: Academic Press, 1973). I highly recommend this article for the reader who is interested in exploring research on physical attractiveness in greater detail.

2 N. Cavior and D. A. Lombardi, "Developmental Aspects of Judgment of Physical Attractiveness in Children," *Developmental Psychology*, 1973, 8, 67–71.

3 J. F. Cross and J. Cross, "Age, Sex, Race, and the Perception of Facial Beauty," *Developmental Psychology*, 1971, 5, 433–439.

4 A. G. Miller, "Role of Physical Attractiveness in Impression Formation," *Psychonomic Science*, 1970, 19, 241–243.

5 A. G. Miller, "Social Perception of Internal-External Control," *Perceptual and Motor Skills*, 1970, 30, 103–109.

6 D. Byrne, O. London, and K. Reeves, "The Effects of Physical Attractiveness, Sex, and Attitude Similarity on Interpersonal Attraction," *Journal of Personality*, 1968, 36, 259–271.

7 W. Stroebe, C. A. Insko, V. D. Thompson, and B. D. Layton, "Effects of Physical Attractiveness, Attitude Similarity, and Sex on Various Aspects of Interpersonal Attraction," *Journal of Personality and Social Psychology*, 1971, 18, 79–91.

8 K. K. Dion, E. Berscheid, and E. Walster, "What is Beautiful is Good," *Journal of Personality and Social Psychology*, 1973, 24, 285–290.

9 F. Monahan, *Women in Crime* (New York: Ives Washburn, 1941).

10 D. Landy and H. Sigall, "Beauty is Talent: Task Evaluation as a Function of the Performer's Physical Attractiveness," *Journal of Personality and Social Psychology*, 1974, 29, 299–304.

11 K. K. Dion and E. Berscheid, "Physical Attractiveness and Peer Perception Among Children," *Sociometry*, 1974, 37, 1–12.

12 M. M. Clifford and E. Walster, "The Effect of Physical Attractiveness on Teacher Expectation," *Sociology of Education*, 1973, 46, 248–258.

13 E. Berscheid and E. Walster, "Physical Attractiveness."

14 *Ibid.*

15 K. K. Dion, "Physical Attractiveness and Evaluations of Children's Transgressions," *Journal of Personality and Social Psychology*, 1972, 24, 207–213.

16 E. Walster, V. Aronson, D. Abrahams, and L. Rottmann, "Importance of Physical Attractiveness in Dating Behavior," *Journal of Personality and Social Psychology*, 1966, 4, 508–516.

17 R. W. Brislin and S. A. Lewis, "Dating and Physical Attractiveness: Replication," *Psychological Reports*, 1968, 22, 976.

18 A. Tesser and M. Brodie, "A Note on the Evaluation of a 'Computer Date,' " *Psychonomic Science*, 1971, 23, 300.

19 D. Byrne, C. R. Ervin, and J. Lamberth, "Continuity Between the Experimental Study of Attraction and Real-Life Computer Dating," *Journal of Personality and Social Psychology*, 1970, 16, 157–165.

20 J. Mills and E. Aronson, "Opinion Change as a Function of the Communicator's Attractiveness and Desire to Influence," *Journal of Personality and Social Psychology*, 1965, 1, 173–177.

21 H. Sigall and E. Aronson, "Liking for an Evaluator as a Function of Her

Physical Attractiveness and Nature of the Evaluations," *Journal of Experimental Social Psychology*, 1969, 5, 93–100.

22 H. SIGALL and D. LANDY, "Radiating Beauty: The Effects of Having a Physically Attractive Partner on Person Perception," *Journal of Personality and Social Psychology*, 1973, 28, 218–224.

23 F. A. PERRIN, "Physical Attractiveness and Repulsiveness," *Journal of Experimental Psychology*, 1921, 4, 203–217.

24 G. THORNTON, "The Effect of Wearing Glasses upon Judgments of Personality Traits of Persons Seen Briefly," *Journal of Applied Psychology*, 1944, 28, 203–207.

25 W. MCKEACHIE, "Lipstick as a Determiner of First Impressions of Personality: An Experiment for the General Psychology Course," *Journal of Social Psychology*, 1952, 36, 241–244.

26 D. G. FREEDMAN, "The Survival Value of the Beard," *Psychology Today*, 1969, 3, 36–39.

27 R. J. PELLEGRINI, "Impressions of the Male Personality as a Function of Beardedness," *Psychology*, 1973, 10, 29–33.

28 R. HOULT, "Experimental Measurement of Clothing as a Factor in Some Social Ratings of Selected American Men," *American Sociological Review*, 1954, 19, 324–328.

29 J. KELLEY, "Dress as Nonverbal Communication," Paper presented to the Annual Conference of the American Association for Public Opinion Research, May, 1969. This study is discussed by M. L. Knapp in *Nonverbal Communication in Human Interaction* (New York: Holt, 1972), p. 83.

30 M. LEFKOWITZ, R. BLAKE, and J. MOUTON, "Status Factors in Pedestrian Violation of Traffic Signals," *Journal of Abnormal and Social Psychology*, 1955, 51, 704–706.

31 L. BICKMAN, "The Effect of Social Status on the Honesty of Others," *Journal of Social Psychology*, 1971, 85, 87–92.

32 R. D. COURSEY, "Clothes Doth Make the Man, in the Eye of the Beholder," *Perceptual and Motor Skills*, 1973, 36, 1259–1264.

33 P. HAMID, "Changes in Perception as a Function of Dress," *Perceptual and Motor Skills*, 1969, 29, 191–194.

34 S. A. RICHARDSON, N. GOODMAN, A. H. HASTORF, and S. M. DORNBUSCH, "Cultural Uniformity in Reactions to Physical Disabilities," *American Sociological Review*, 1961, 26, 241–247.

35 N. GOODMAN, S. M. DORNBUSCH, S. A. RICHARDSON, and A. H. HASTORF, "Variant Reactions to Physical Disabilities," *American Sociological Review*, 1968, 28, 429–435.

36 W. WELLS and B. SIEGEL, "Stereotyped Somatypes," *Psychological Reports*, 1961, 8, 77–78.

37 K. T. STRONGMAN and C. J. HART, "Stereotyped Reactions to Body Build," *Psychological Reports*, 1968, 23, 1175–1178.

38 J. R. Staffieri, "A Study of Social Sterotypes of Body Image in Children," *Journal of Personality and Social Psychology*, 1967, 7, 101-104.

39 R. M. Lerner and E. Gellert, "Body Build Identification, Preference, and Aversion in Children," *Developmental Psychology*, 1969, 1, 456-462.

40 R. M. Lerner, "The Development of Stereotyped Expectations of Body Build-Behavior Relations," *Child Development*, 1969, 40,137-141.

41 W. J. Cahnman, "The Stigma of Obesity," *Sociological Quarterly*, 1968, 9, 283-299.

42 W. J. Cahnman.

43 S. M. Jourard and P. F. Secord, "Body-Cathexis and the Ideal Female Figure," *Journal of Abnormal and Social Psychology*, 1955, 50, 243-246.

44 M. L. Knapp, *Nonverbal Communication in Human Interaction* (New York: Holt, Rinehart, & Winston, 1972), p. 73.

45 *Ibid.*

46 P. R. Wilson, "Perceptual Distortion of Height as a Function of Ascribed Academic Status," *Journal of Social Psychology*, 1968, 74, 97-102.

47 W. D. Dannenmaier, and F. J. Thumain, "Authority Status as a Factor in Perceptual Distortion of Size," *Journal of Social Psychology*, 1964, 63, 361-365.

48 H. H. Kassarjian, "Voting Intention and Political Perception," *Journal of Psychology*, 1963, 56, 85-88.

49 C. Ward, "Own Height, Sex, and Liking in the Judgment of the Heights of Others," *Journal of Personality*, 1967, 35, 381-401.

50 D. Koulack and J. A. Tuthill, "Height Perception: A Function of Social Distance," *Canadian Journal of Behavioral Science*, 1972, 4, 50-53.

51 H. R. Stolz and L. M. Stolz, *Somatic Development of Adolescent Boys* (New York: Macmillan, 1951).

52 E. Aronson, "Some Antecedents of Interpersonal Attraction," *Nebraska Symposium on Motivation* (Lincoln: University of Nebraska Press, 1969).

53 Berscheid and Walster, "Physical Attractiveness."

54 H. L. Miller and W. H. Riverbank, "Sexual Differences in Physical Attractiveness as a Determinant of Heterosexual Likings," *Phychological Reports*, 1970, 27, 701-702.

55 N. Cavior, "Physical Attractiveness, Perceived Attitude Similarity, and Interpersonal Attraction Among Fifth and Eleventh Grade Boys and Girls," Doctoral dissertation, University of Houston, 1970. This research is summarized by Berscheid and Walster.

56. R. L. Kurtzberg, H. Safar, and N. Cavior, "Surgical and Social Rehabilitation of Adult Offenders," *Proceedings of the 76th Annual Convention of the American Psychological Association*, 1968, 3, 649-650. This research is summarized by Berscheid and Walster.

57 P. H. Secord and S. M. Jourard, "The Appraisal of Body-Cathexis: Body-Cathexis and the Self," *Journal of Consulting Psychology*, 1953, 17, 343-347.

58 BERSCHEID and WALSTER, "Physical Attractiveness."

59 *Ibid.*

60 F. A. PERRIN, "Physical Attractiveness and Repulsiveness."

61 BERSCHEID and WALSTER, "Physical Attractiveness."

62 M. L. KNAPP, *Nonverbal Communication in Human Interaction.*

2

I Could Tell by the Look in His/Her Eyes

The following ad appeared in a Boston underground newspaper:

Beautiful woman, you boarded MTA at Central Sq. May 20, 1 p.m. You had gold shawl, violet jersey, long white print dress, sandals, large leather bag, soft brown curls, striking eyes in gray textbook. You looked up. I had curly brown hair, glasses, mustache, cord jacket, umbrella, blue valise. Our eyes met four times. I'd like to try it again. This time with words.

Apparently the man who placed the ad interpreted the four instances of eye contact as a sign that he and the young lady were interested in each other. We know from our own experience that we can communicate our attraction toward people by gazing at them. Those wishing to reciprocate our interest can return their gaze toward us. People who are not attracted can show this by looking away. But looking at people is not always taken as a sign of positive attraction. We have all been in the situation of looking at somebody longer than "allowed" and being confronted with the blunt question, "What are you looking at?" Some of you may have heard or used the expression "Take a picture, it lasts longer." The way in which our gaze is interpreted depends so much on the situation and the particular individuals involved that it is difficult to give a general rule for predicting when looking at someone will be taken positively and when it will be received negatively. In hostile or competitive interactions between people, gaze seems to accentuate unpleasant feelings. In friendly and cooperative interactions between people, gaze is often found to increase positive feelings. Let us examine some of the different ways in which gazing behavior has been studied. You will be able to see how the effects of gaze have been found to vary in the different contexts and situations which were investiga ed.

GAZE AND DISCOMFORT

When we are uncomfortable with or dislike another person, we often avoid giving gaze. Receiving gaze from someone else can also be aversive, especially when it communicates threat or dominance. Most of you are familiar with the writings of animal researchers who have interpreted gaze as a display of aggression or threat and gaze aversion as a sign of submission. One investigator found that by staring at monkeys he could elicit behaviors of anger and attack.[1]

A number of studies have shown that autistic and schizophrenic persons look significantly less at others than average people do. This avoidance of eye contact has been interpreted as an attempt to withdraw from interaction with other people, which to the autistic and schizophrenic person is emotionally arousing and uncomfortable.[2,3,4]

College students have been found to look much less at an interviewer when the interview questions are about embarrassing issues than when the interview questions are about nonembarrassing issues.[5] Participants in one experiment were either criticized or praised by an experimenter. The participants who were praised showed an increase in eye contact with the experimenter during the course of the experiment. The participants who were criticized decreased their eye contact with the experimenter.[6]

As with animals, gaze between humans can serve as a sign of dominance or competition. Alexander Solzhenitsyn gives an insightful description of the operation of gaze in interpersonal conflict:[7]

Zoya's stare, ready to rebuff her, was so bold that Vera Kornilyevna realized that it would be impossible for her to prove anything and Zoya had already decided as much. Zoya's rebuff and her determination were so strong that Vera Kornilyevna couldn't understand them. She lowered her eyes.

She always lowered her eyes when she was thinking unpleasant thoughts about someone.

She lowered her eyes guiltily while Zoya, having won the battle, continued to test her with her straightforward gaze.

Zoya had won the battle . . .

The relationship between gaze and dominance between people has also been studied by experimental psychologists. Male students were introduced to another male who gazed at them very often or very little. The students who received extended gaze from the other person saw him as being significantly more dominant than the students who received only brief gaze.[8] In another study, male students were angered by another male and then were given an opportunity to vent their anger by giving shocks to him. The angered students gave significantly fewer shocks when the person who had angered them gazed at them steadily than when he did not gaze. The students reported that being gazed at by the person who had angered them was very discomforting and that they did not shock him so often because by not shocking him they could avoid his gaze.[9]

An example of how gaze can serve as an aversive stimulus which people attempt to escape is shown in a recent field experiment conducted in California. Men and women drivers waiting at a red traffic light were confronted by a person who stared at them until the light turned green. Sometimes the staring person was on a motor scooter and sometimes the staring person was standing on the corner. Drivers who were stared at crossed the intersection with significantly greater speed after the light turned green than another group of drivers who were not stared at. Both male and female drivers showed the same motivation to escape from staring men as well as from staring women.[10]

GAZE AND PHYSIOLOGICAL AROUSAL

In some situations physiological responses are influenced by gaze from another person. The galvanic skin response of men and women was found to be higher when they looked at someone who was gazing back at them than when they looked at someone who looked away.[11] Galvanic skin response is a measure of skin resistance and how much we are perspiring. A high galvanic skin response means that the skin is damp and its resistance is low. This is often interpreted as an index of emotional arousal. In another study, college men played a competitive game with a male opponent who either gazed at them constantly or not at all. The men who received constant gaze from their opponent had significantly higher heart rates than the men receiving no gaze.[12] Certain brain waves have also been shown to be affected by how much gaze a person receives.[13] It isn't possible to state precisely what all of these physiological responses mean, but it was concluded in the above studies that gaze served as a stimulus to increase emotional arousal.

GAZE AND POSITIVE FEELING

We have seen that gaze from another person in competitive situations is likely to be interpreted as expressing hostility or dominance. In a friendly or relaxed social context we tend instead to use gaze as a measure of how much people like each other. The relationship between gaze and positive feeling has been studied in a variety of different ways.

Gaze in Videotapes. Two groups of investigators measured the reactions of people to various amounts of gaze in videotapes. In one study, men and women observed videotapes in which instructions for an experiment were read by a male who either never looked up at the camera or looked up twice. The men and women participants rated the experimenter in the videotapes as less formal and less nervous when he looked up than when he did not look up.[14] Another study had actors portray the role of engaged couples in a videotaped interview. In half of the videotapes the "engaged" couples gazed at each other fairly often during the interview. In the other videotapes the couples never looked at each other. College students who viewed the videotapes and rated the couples were led to believe that the interviews were genuine and that the couples were actually engaged. Couples who gazed at each other were rated as significantly more genuine, relaxed, cooperative, intelligent, and attentive toward each other than couples who did not gaze. In addition, couples who gazed at each other were seen as liking each other more, as having better potential for a successful marriage, and were rated as better liked by the viewers than couples who did not gaze.[15]

Liking People Who Gaze. You've heard this said in seriousness:

I know he/she liked me. I could tell by the way he/she looked at me.

Others put it more humorously:

I know he/she liked me. I could tell by the way I looked at him/her.

We often get an impression of how much people like us by the amount that they look at us. College men and women who arrived to participate in a psychology experiment were introduced briefly to two other people and asked privately to choose which of the two they would prefer to have as a partner during the experiment. Both of the people to whom the participants were introduced were actually confederates of the experimenter and were trained in such a way that one would maintain eye contact with the participant during the introduction and one would look away. Results showed that both men and women participants were significantly more likely to choose the person who looked at them during the introduction. The confederates took turns looking and not looking to show that it was their gaze and not their appearance which made the difference in whether or not they were chosen as a partner.[16]

Males and females were asked to talk briefly about an interesting event in their lives to a listener who either leaned forward and gazed a lot or leaned back and rarely gazed. The males and females were more likely to look at listeners who looked at them. They also stated that they preferred the listeners who leaned forward and gazed over the listeners who leaned back and did not gaze.[17]

A female experimenter gave a brief speech to a number of pairs of female undergraduate students. The experimenter arranged it so that during her talk she would look at one of the students 90 percent of the time and the other student 10 percent of the time. When students were questioned afterwards they stated that the student who had received the most gaze from the experimenter appeared to be liked best by her.[18]

Females who interviewed males about their interests and hobbies were rated by the males as significantly more attentive if they gazed at a high rather than a low level. Males also gave significantly briefer answers to females who did not gaze at them, compared with females who gazed at them all of the time or half of the time.[19]

Whether or not we like someone who gazes often depends on the context in which the gazing is done. Women students were interviewed individually by a female who either looked at them very often during the interview or hardly at all. In addition, for half of the participants the content of the interview was positive and complimentary and for the other participants it was negative and threatening. When asked to give their reactions toward the interviewer the students who had the positive interview preferred the interviewer when she gazed. Students who were in the negative interview, on the other hand, preferred the interviewer when she did not gaze.[20] A similar study found that a male experimenter who gave a personal evaluation to men and women was liked most if he did not gaze very much. When giving an impersonal evaluation, the experimenter was evaluated most favorably if he gazed quite often.[21]

The effects of gazing can also depend on the physical attractiveness of the person who gazes. Male and female students were introduced to each other and left alone to talk about anything they chose for fifteen minutes. The females were actually confederates in the experiment and were trained to gaze at their male partners either 90 percent of the time or 10 percent of the time. If the females were physically attractive it did not make much difference whether their gaze during the conversation was high or low. Unattractive females, on the other hand, were rated much more negatively by their partners when their gaze was low. Overall, attractive females were favored by males over unattractive females.[22]

When We Like to Gaze. Besides judging people's liking by their gaze toward us, we can also communicate our liking for others by how much we gaze at them. It has been found that people gaze more when approaching a coat-rack and pretending it is a person whom they like rather than dislike.[23,24] Female students who came into an experiment were told that they would be introduced to a female interviewer. Half of the students were given the instructions that they should try to gain friendship with the interviewer. The other students were instructed to attempt to avoid friendship with the interviewer. Students who were trying to make friends with the interviewer gazed at her significantly more than students who wanted to avoid her friendship.[25]

In addition to gazing most at people we like, we also gaze more at people when they are attentive or polite toward us. Male students were asked to talk briefly to two other male listeners. One of the listeners gave approval with smiles and head nods while the other listener appeared interested but gave no approval. The students perceived the listener who gave approval as liking them more than the neutral listener and they gazed significantly more at the approving listener during their talk.[26,27] People have been found to increase their eye contact with an interviewer who evaluates them positively and decrease their eye contact with an interviewer who evaluates them negatively. People also gaze more at interviewers whom they like than at interviewers whom they dislike.[28]

Eye contact between dating couples who were very close was compared with eye contact between dating couples who were not so close. It turned out that the close couples looked at each other significantly more often than did the couples who were less close.[29]

GAZE, HONESTY, AND PERSUASION

The amount of time that we look at someone when speaking is sometimes interpreted as communicating how truthful we are. The admonishment often given to children, "Look at me when you are speaking!" is familiar to all of us. When people are asked to tell a lie they look less at their audience than when they are asked to tell the truth.[30] When people want to be persuasive they look at their audience more.[31] People tend to judge verbal statements as more credible when they ae accompanied with gaze.[32]

A group of female college students went to airports and shopping centers and asked people to do them various favors, such as mailing a letter or lending a dime. Half of the time the females looked directly at the person when asking the favor and half of the time they looked down or off to the side. The differences were not remarkable, but in all cases people were more willing to comply with the requests of females who gazed than with those of females who looked away.[33]

DIFFERENCES BETWEEN MEN AND WOMEN

Research has shown fairly consistently that women tend to look more and give more eye contact than men. This might be because women are generally more open to intimacy than men or because of a greater desire by women to seek feedback about how others are reacting toward them.[34]

Male and female college students were introduced in pairs and left alone in a room to talk about anything they chose for ten minutes. After ten minutes, a male experimenter came into the room and told the couple that he had been measuring through a hidden one-way mirror how much one of them had looked at the other during the conversation. Half of the time the experimenter had supposedly measured how much the male looked at the female and half of the time the measure was supposedly of how much the female had looked at the male. The experimenter told the couple that the amount of time the one person had looked at the other was significantly longer than most people look, about average, or significantly shorter. This feedback had nothing to do with how much the people had actually looked, but was designed to influence the perceptions that the participants had of their own looking behavior or the looking behavior of their partner. The false feedback about gaze was believable to the participants because there actually was a one-way mirror in the room and because most of us aren't aware enough of how much we look at people to question the feedback of an experimenter. The point of all this discussion is that females reacted most positively when they thought they or their partner had gazed at a very high level. Males, on the other hand, were not comfortable with the idea that they might have given or received above average amounts of gaze. Males reacted most positively when they thought their gaze or the gaze of their partner was average.[35]

PUPIL SIZE

Eckhard Hess tells the story that he and his wife were in bed reading one night when he happened to notice that his wife's pupils changed size as she came to different parts of her book. It occurred to Hess that pupil size might have something to do with one's interest or favor in whatever he or she is looking at. As a result of Hess' insight, a number of studies have been conducted showing that pupil sizes increase when people are looking at favorable or positive stimuli. Pupils of males become larger when they are looking at pictures of nude females.[36,37,38] People looking at slides of political figures have larger pupils when the picture is of someone they like and smaller pupils when the picture is of someone they dislike.[39] Homosexual and heterosexual males have been differentiated by showing that homosexuals have larger pupils when looking at pictures of men.[40]

Hess also investigated whether or not pupil size would have any influence on first impressions. People were asked to give their reactions to an attractive woman in two photographs which were identical in all aspects but one. In one of the photographs the woman's pupils had been made to look slightly larger. Hess found that people preferred the woman when her pupils were large.[41]

An interesting study of pupil size was conducted with people in a real interaction. Participants came to take part in an experiment and were asked privately to choose one of two people as their partner. One of the people had pupils which were dilated with a drug. The other person had normal pupils. When choosing between two females, both men and women participants favored the female with enlarged pupils. When choosing between two males, both men and women participants preferred the male with enlarged pupils. Care was taken to vary which male or female stimulus people would have enlarged and normal pupils in order to be certain that it was really pupil size and not other factors, such as relative attractiveness or unattractiveness, which influenced the participants' choices.[42]

TO GAZE OR NOT TO GAZE

You can see now why I said earlier that it is impossible to state precisely when gaze will be interpreted favorably and when it will be interpreted unfavorably. The effects of gaze depend on factors having to do with the situation and the person who is gazing who is gazing which are too complex at this point to define. In some situations, and in the association of some facial expressions, gaze can be an aversive stimulus. In other contexts, gaze can be a sign of attraction and liking. It is possible that gaze serves mainly to accentuate whatever feelings are present in a given situation. In a pleasant encounter gaze might increase the pleasantness and in an unpleasant encounter gaze might function to increase feelings of discomfort. You may be interested in seeing what happens when you gaze or do not gaze at various people you encounter. Try observing other people and see when and how much they look at each other. But don't blame me if they ask you what you're looking at!

NOTES

1 R. V. Exline, "Visual Interaction," *Nebraska Symposium on Motivation*, 1971 (Lincoln: University of Nebraska Press), pp. 163–206.

2 C. Hutt and C. Ounstead, "The Biological Significance of Gaze Aversion With Particular Reference to the Syndrome of Infantile Autism," *Behavioral Science*, 1966, 11, 346–356.

3 H. M. Lefcourt, F. Rotenberg, R. Buckspan, and R. Steffy, "Visual Interaction and Performance of Process and Reactive Schizophrenics as a Function of Examiner's Sex," *Journal of Personality*, 1967, 35, 535–546.

4 D. R. Rutter and G. M. Stephenson, "Visual Interaction in a Group of Schizophrenic and Depressive Patients," *British Journal of Social and Clinical Psychology*, 1972, 11, 57–65.

5 R. V. Exline, D. Gray, and D. Schuette, "Visual Behavior in a Dyad as Affected by Interview Content and Sex of Respondent," *Journal of Personality and Social Psychology*, 1965, 1, 201–209.

6 A. Modigliani, "Embarrassment, Facework, and Eye-Contact: Testing a Theory of Embarrassment," *Journal of Personality and Social Psychology*, 1971, 17, 15–24.

7 A. SOLZHENITSYN, *Cancer Ward* (New York: Bantam Books, 1969), pp. 370–371.

8 S. THAYER, "The Effect of Interpersonal Looking Duration on Dominance Judgments," *Journal of Social Psychology*, 1969, 79, 285–286.

9 P. C. ELLSWORTH and J. M. CARLSMITH, "Eye Contact and Gaze Aversion in an Aggressive Encounter," *Journal of Personality and Social Psychology*, 1973, 28, 280–292.

10 P. C. ELLSWORTH, J. M. CARLSMITH, and A. HENSON, "The Stare as a Stimulus to Flight in Human Subjects: A Series of Field Experiments," *Journal of Personality and Social Psychology*, 1972, 21, 302–311.

11 K. A. NICHOLS and B. G. CHAMPNESS, "Eye Gaze and the GSR," *Journal of Experimental Social Psychology*, 1971, 7, 623–626.

12 C. L. KLEINKE and P. D. POHLEN, "Affective and Emotional Responses as a Function of Other Person's Gaze and Cooperativeness in a Two-Person Game," *Journal of Personality and Social Psychology*, 1971, 17, 308–313.

13 A. GALE, B. LUCAS, R. NISSIM, and B. HARPHAM, "Some EEG Correlates of Face-To-Face Contact," *British Journal of Social and Clinical Psychology*, 1972, 11, 326–332.

14 W. F. LeCOMPTE and H. M. ROSENFELD, "Effects of Minimal Eye Contact in the Instruction Period on Impressions of the Experimenter," *Journal of Experimental Social Psychology*, 1971, 7, 211–220.

15 C. L. KLEINKE, F. B. MEEKER, and C. La FONG, "Effects of Gaze, Touch, and Use of Name on Evaluation of 'Engaged' Couples," *Journal of Research in Personality*, 1974, 7, 368–373.

16 J. W. STASS and F. N. WILLIS, "Eye-Contact, Pupil Dilation, and Personal Preference," *Psychonomic Science*, 1967, 7, 375–376.

17 G. BREED, "The Effect of Intimacy: Reciprocity or Retreat?" *British Journal of Social and Clinical Psychology*, 1972, 11, 135–142.

18 A. MEHRABIAN, "Orientation Behaviors and Nonverbal Attitude Communication," *Journal of Communication*, 1967, 17, 324–332.

19 C. L. KLEINKE, R. A. STANESKI, and D. E. BERGER, "Evaluation of an Interviewer as a Function of Interviewer Gaze, Reinforcement of Subject Gaze, and Interviewer Attractiveness," *Journal of Personality and Social Psychology*, 1975, 31, 115–122.

20 P. C. ELLSWORTH and J. M. CARLSMITH, "Effects of Eye-Contact and Verbal Content on Affective Responses to a Dyadic Interaction," *Journal of Personality and Social Psychology*, 1968, 10, 15–20.

21 L. SCHERWITZ and R. HELMREICH, "Interactive Effects of Eye Contact and Verbal Content on Interpersonal Attraction in Dyads," *Journal of Personality and Social Psychology*, 1973, 25, 6–14.

22 C. L. KLEINKE, R. A. STANESKI, and S. L. PIPP, "Effects of Gaze, Distance, and Attractiveness on Males' First Impressions of Females," *Representative Research in Social Psychology*, 1975, 6, 7–12.

23 A. MEHRABIAN, "Inference of Attitude From the Posture, Orientation, and

Distance of a Communicator," *Journal of Consulting and Clinical Psychology*, 1968, 32, 296–308.
24 A. MEHRABIAN, "Relationship of Attitude to Seated Posture, Orientation, and Distance," *Journal of Personality and Social Psychology*, 1968, 10, 26–30.
25 R. J. PELLEGRINI, R. A. HICKS, and L. GORDON, "The Effect of an Approval-Seeking Induction on Eye-Contact in Dyads," *British Journal of Social and Clinical Psychology*, 1970, 9, 373–374.
26 J. S. EFRAN, "Looking for Approval: Effects on Visual Behavior of Approbation From Persons Differing in Importance," *Journal of Personality and Social Psychology*, 1968, 10, 21–25.
27 J. S. EFRAN and A. BROUGHTON, "Effect of Expectancies for Social Approval on Visual Behavior," *Journal of Personality and Social Psychology*, 1966, 4, 103–107.
28 R. V. EXLINE and L. C. WINTERS, "Affective Relations and Mutual Glances in Dyads," in S. S. Tompkins and C. E. Izard (Eds.), *Affect, Cognition, and Personality* (New York: Springer, 1965).
29 Z. RUBIN, "Measurement of Romantic Love," *Journal of Personality and Social Psychology*, 1970, 16, 265–273.
30 A. MEHRABIAN, "Nonverbal Betrayal of Feeling," *Journal of Experimental Research in Personality*, 1971, 5, 64–73.
31 A. MEHRABIAN and M. WILLIAMS, "Nonverbal Concomitants of Perceived and Intended Persuasiveness," *Journal of Personality and Social Psychology*, 1969, 13, 37–58.
32 R. V. EXLINE, "Visual Interaction," p. 199.
33 C. L. KLEINKE, "Compliance to Requests Made by Gazing and Touching Experimenters in Field Settings," *Journal of Experimental Social Psychology*, in press.
34 P. C. ELLSWORTH and L. M. LUDWIG, "Visual Behavior in Social Interaction," *Journal of Communication*, 1972, 22, 375–403.
35 C. L. KLEINKE, A. A. BUSTOS, F. B. MEEKER, and R. A. STANESKI, "Effects of Self-Attributed and Other-Attributed Gaze on Inter-Personal Evaluations Between Males and Females," *Journal of Experimental Social Psychology*, 1973, 9, 154–163.
36 E. H. HESS and J. M. POLT, "Pupil Size as Related to Interest Value of Visual Stimuli," *Science*, 1960, 132, 349–350.
37 J. C. NUNNALLY, P. D. KNOTT, A. DUCHNOWSKI, and R. PARKER, "Pupillary Response as a General Measure of Activation," *Perception and Psychophysics*, 1967, 2, 149–155.
38 L. J. CHAPMAN, J. P. CHAPMAN, and T. BRELJE, "Influence of the Experimenter on Pupillary Dilation to Sexually Provocative Pictures," *Journal of Abnormal Psychology*, 1969, 74, 369–400.
39 J. D. BARLOW, "Pupillary Size as an Index of Preference in Political Candidates," *Perceptual and Motor Skills*, 1969, 28, 587–590.
40 E. H. HESS, A. L. SELTZER, and J. M. SHLIEN, "Pupil Response of Hetero- and

Homosexual Males to Pictures of Men and Women: A Pilot Study," *Journal of Abnormal Psychology*, 1965, 70, 165–168.

41 E. H. HESS, "Attitude and Pupil Size," *Scientific American*, 1965, 212, 46–54.

42 J. W. STASS and F. N. WILLIS, "Eye-Contact, Pupil Dilation, and Personal Preference."

3

The Nearness of You

Anthropologists often tell the story of how foreign participants at international conventions are struck by the fact that Americans seem to prefer holding their conversations near walls and in corners. The reason for this is that the foreign participants often like to stand closer to other people than Americans do. When they are talking with Americans they come to the distance most comfortable to them. The Americans then back away to the distance most comfortable to them. The foreigners again come closer and the Americans again back away. Before long, they have waltzed each other into the corner.

THE LANGUAGE OF DISTANCE

We learn a great deal about people from our observations of interpersonal distance. Theodore H. White gives the following description in his book *The Making of the President, 1960*:

Kennedy loped into the cottage with his light, dancing step, as young and lithe as springtime, and called a greeting to those who stood in his way. Then he seemed to slip from them as he descended the steps of the split-level cottage to a corner where his brother Bobby and brother-in-law Sargent Shriver were chatting, waiting for him. The others in the room surged forward on impulse to join him. Then they halted. A distance of perhaps 30 feet separated them from him, but it was impassable. They stood apart, these older men of long-established power, and watched him. He turned after a few minutes, saw them watching him, and whispered to his brother-in-law. Shriver now crossed the separating space to invite them over. First Averell Harriman; then Dick Daley; then Mike DiSalle, then, one by one, let them all congratulate him. Yet no one could pass the little open distance between him and them uninvited, because there was this thin separation about him, and the knowledge they were there not as his patrons but as his clients. They could come by invitation only, for this might be a President of the United States.[1]

Films were made showing a man at a desk doing some work and then speaking on the phone. Another man then knocks on the door, enters, and approaches the man seated at the desk. The man at the desk brings out some papers and a brief conversation takes place. When people are asked to rate the relative status of the two men, the man who comes into the room is consistently rated subordinate if he stops just inside the door and converses from that distance. The longer it takes the man at the desk to respond to the knock the more status he is given.[2]

Participants in a study looked at a photograph of five college women seated at a rectangular table, apparently in a discussion. One woman sat at the head of the table and two women sat at each side. When asked to give their impressions of the women, college students rated the one at the head of the table as more talkative, persuasive, dominant, self-confident, intelligent, and as more of a leader, compared with the other four women. The position of the women at the table was different for different raters in order to control for the effects of physical appearance.[3] Groups which were set up as mock juries showed a significant tendency to choose the person sitting at the head of the table as the leader.[4]

You know from your own experience that college professors and company presidents are associated with sitting at the head of the table. When people are questioned about seating arrangements, they reserve the head of a table for high-status persons.[5]

SPACE INFLUENCES OUR BEHAVIOR

The ways in which we behave often have a lot to do with environmental factors or space and distance that surround us. We have seen that people sitting at heads of tables are most often identified as leaders. It is true, in addition, that people who are sitting at heads of tables (even if by chance) often *feel* and *act* more like leaders.[6,7]

In his book *Personal Space*, Robert Sommer talks about how space and distance can affect behaviors in places such as hospitals, classrooms, bars, and hotels. It has been shown, for example, that conversations and interactions among people are strongly influenced by the seating arrangements of the room in which they find themselves. The seating arrangement in the dayroom of a home for the elderly was changed from one in which chairs and couches stood against the walls to one in which chairs were placed around tables. As a result of the new seating arrangement, social interactions between the residents of the home nearly doubled.[8]

Carol Holahan compared the effects of several different seating arrangements in the dayroom of a psychiatric hospital. When the chairs were arranged around tables there was significantly more social interaction between patients and significantly more patient satisfaction and rapport than when the chairs were placed against the walls.[9] The implications of the effects of space on behavior are important:

> The finding that dayroom seating arrangements exert significant influence over patients' social behavior is most important in the light of the tendency of many professional mental health workers and of the public to attribute the psychiatric patient's behavior entirely to psychodynamic factors within himself. The most common response of the ward nurses in this hospital on being told of this study was that chair arrangements would not affect patients' social functioning. "The patients may sit at the tables," one nurse responded confidently, "but they won't talk to one another." [10]

It is obvious that seating arrangements *can* affect behavior. Sommer and Holahan both feel that seating arrangements in therapeutic settings should be geared toward the needs of the residents rather than the convenience of the staff.

Space influences how we react toward and interact with other people. Males and females were brought into a seven-by-nine-foot room to fill out a series of questionnaires. For half of the participants the temperature in the room was a comfortable 73 degrees. The other participants were subjected to a relatively uncomfortable 93.5 degrees. Sometimes there were only three to five participants in the room. At other times the number of participants in the room was between twelve and sixteen. After the participants had been in the room for forty-five minutes they were asked to look at a rating form filled out by someone they did not know and give their evaluation of that person. Participants were significantly less favorable toward the stranger when the room they were in was hot and when the room they were in was crowded.[11] In other studies it has been found that people are much more favorable in their evaluations of others when they are making their evaluations in an attractively decorated room rather than in an unattractive room.[12,13]

Psychiatric patients were interviewed by therapists at one of three distances: three feet, six feet, or nine feet. Patients were significantly more anxious and had most difficulty in getting their point across when the therapist sat far away from them rather than close to them. Patients talked more openly about themselves when they were at a distance of six feet. Therapists all stated that they preferred the distance of six feet.[14]

WHEN PEOPLE COME CLOSE TO US

Formation of Impressions. We all feel positively about being physically close to people we know well and like. How do we feel about strangers who come close to us?

Participants in a study of first impressions were interviewed by a male or female who sat either two, four, six, or eight feet away from them. After the interview, participants gave their impressions of the interviewer. Interviewers who sat at a distance of four feet were rated as most friendly and most socially active. It was thought that the interviewers might have communicated signs of discomfort when they had to sit as close as two feet from the people they interviewed.[15]

Males and females were introduced in pairs and left in a room for fifteen minutes to talk about anything they wished. The original distance between the participants was forty-five inches. After five minutes, the female either moved her chair (which had wheels) closer to the male to a distance of twenty-nine inches or farther from the male to a distance of sixty-eight inches. This movement was made as casually as possible and took about a minute or so to complete. When interviewed after the conversation the males stated that they had noticed the movement of the females but did not feel that it affected any of their impressions or reactions toward her. Whether or not a male liked a female depended primarily on her attractiveness.[16]

Invasions of Personal Space. Some investigators conceive of people as possessing a sort of body buffer zone. When others come closer than this zone allows it causes discomfort. Schizophrenics and prisoners have a wide buffer zone and prefer to keep farther distances from others than average people do.[17,18,19] The galvanic skin response of people has been measured as they are approached by others from different directions. Frontal approach causes the most emotional arousal. A side approach produces less arousal than a frontal approach and more arousal than an approach from the rear. Emotional arousal is greater when the approaching other is of the opposite sex and when the person being approached is touched by another person rather than by an object.[20]

Robert Sommer discusses a number of studies in which experimenters measured the reactions of other people when their personal space had been invaded. Typically, experimenters would come up and sit next to people on park benches or in a library and measure how much time went by until the person would get up and leave. People whose personal space was invaded showed signs of discomfort and departed from where they were sitting much sooner than other people in the same situation whose personal space was not invaded.[21,22]

College students who were angered by an experimenter later came significantly closer when asked to approach the experimenter than students who had not been angered by the experimenter. The sex of the student or experimenter did not make a difference. It was concluded that the students who were angered by the experimenter were retaliating by invading the experimenter's personal space.[23]

Sommer gives the following description of how close distances are used in police interrogations to invade a suspect's personal space:

> One police textbook recommends that the interrogator should sit close to the suspect, with no table or desk between them, since "an obstruction of any sort affords the subject a certain degree of relief and confidence not otherwise attainable." At the beginning of the session, the officer's chair may be two or three feet away, "but after the interrogation is under way the interrogator should move his chair in closer so that ultimately one of the subject's knees is just about in between the interrogator's two knees." [24]

Compliance and Agreement. Interpersonal distance can affect the way in which we respond to the arguments or requests of another person. Male students were given a five-minute argument by a male speaker who sat either one to two feet away, or fourteen to fifteen feet away. The students later showed more agreement with the speaker's position when he had sat far from them rather than close to them. It is possible that the students felt unfairly pressured when the speaker sat close to them.[25] In another study, male students discussed certain issues of contemporary interest with another person who sat either four feet away or ten feet away. The seating distance had nothing to do with whether or not the students would change their final opinions to agree with the other person. During the conversation, however, the students did show more nonverbal agreement with head nods and more arousal with gestures when the other person sat close rather than far. People may not be willing to change their attitudes if a speaker sits very close to them, but they do appear to feel some pressure to at least respond in a social manner.[26]

Male volunteers came into an experiment and were told that the study required them to press a button which would deliver electric shocks to another person who was also a volunteer. In reality the buttons did not deliver shocks, but the participants who were to press them did not know this. The volunteers, of course, expressed doubts about giving shocks to another person, but the experimenter insisted that they do so. It turned out that a large percentage of the participants complied with the experimenter's order. It was also found that the participants would comply a good deal more readily with the order if the experimenter was physically close to them than if the experimenter was farther away or in another room. When the person supposedly delivering the shocks was physically close to the "victim" he gave fewer shocks than when the physical distance between them was great. Participants who had to touch the victims complied with the experimenter's orders only half as often as participants who were supposedly shocking somebody in another room.[27]

WHEN WE PREFER TO COME CLOSE

We come close to people we like and feel comfortable with.

Forty college students carried measuring tapes for several days and recorded the distance to which various people approached them. When students encountered anyone who began a conversation with them they remained at a fixed point. Then, when the other person approached and began to talk, the students took out the measuring tape and measured the resulting nose-to-nose distance. All in all, women students were approached more closely than men students. Both men and women had closer distances to close friends than acquaintances, and to peers rather than older people. Parents did not come nearly as close to the students as did the students' friends.[28]

People come significantly closer when they are asked to approach a coat-rack pretending it is a person whom they like rather than dislike.[29,30,31] People standing close together are seen by observers as liking each other more than people standing far apart.[32]

Female students were instructed either to try to get another female to like them or to avoid friendship with her when they were introduced. Students who wanted to be friendly with the other female sat significantly closer to her after their introduction than students who were motivated not to become friends.[33]

College students were introduced as blind dates. After their date, couples who liked each other a lot stood closer together than couples who did not like each other so much.[34]

College students were asked to specify which other students in a classroom they liked or disliked. It was later found that the students sat closer to people whom they liked and farther from people they disliked.[35]

WHEN WE PREFER TO WITHDRAW

We withdraw from people we dislike and feel uncomfortable with.

Students were put into a situation in which they thought they were either going to be reprimanded or praised by an authority figure. Students expecting to be reprimanded seated themselves significantly farther away from the person of authority than students expecting to be praised.[36]

Male participants in an experiment were led to believe they had done either very well or very poorly on a learning task in comparison with another participant in the same room. Later, it was found that males who had experienced success would come close to the other person. Males who had experienced failure showed a tendency to stay farther away from a person who had done better than they had.[37]

Males and females were asked to approach another person under one of two conditions. Half of the participants were placed under stress by being told that they would be closely evaluated in terms of their attractiveness and appeal as they were approaching the other person. The other participants were in a neutral condition and felt no pressure of evaluation from the person they were to approach. Both males and females kept a significantly greater distance from the other person when they were under the stress of being evaluated than when they were in the neutral situation.[38]

Observations of kindergarten children have shown that when they are friendly they tend to play together at a close distance and when they are unfriendly they increase the distance between one another.[39]

People with physical disabilities suffer not only the disability, but also the avoidance of others with whom they come in contact. College females were asked to teach a task to a male who was made to look as if his left leg had been amputated or who appeared normal. The females stayed significantly farther away from the male when he was made up as an amputee than when he was in a normal condition.[40] Male college students came into an experiment and were introduced to another person with whom they would be working. Half of the time the other person was identified as having epilepsy and half of the time he was given no special identity. When the students were given a chance to sit down, they placed their chairs significantly farther away from the other person when he was identified as an epileptic than when he was perceived as having no special disability.[41]

AVOIDANCE OF A COMMUNICATION GAP

In his books *The Silent Language* and *The Hidden Dimension*, Edward Hall discusses a variety of interesting observations he has made of interpersonal distances in various cultures. Hall's feeling is that barriers may arise between people if they don't understand the differences in the ways they perceive their own and one another's personal space. Studies in the U.S. have shown variations in distance between certain groups of people. A male experimenter taking a poll found that people in the Little Italy section of New York City would stand closer to him than people in Greenwich Village. In addition, people in Little Italy (a conservative area) came significantly closer to the experimenter when he was wearing a button with an American flag rather than a peace button. People in Greenwich Village (a liberal area) came somewhat closer when the experimenter wore the peace button.[42]

Observations of children at a zoo found that Mexican-American children stood closest together, white children maintained intermediate distance, and black children stood farthest apart. Younger children stood closer together than older children and adults. Male-female groups stood closer than female-female and male-male groups.[43] A study of schoolchildren in New York City showed that middle-class white children stood farther apart than lower-class black and Puerto Rican children. These differences in distance were only prevalent for first- and second-graders. By the third grade, children of different races did not differ in interpersonal distance.[44, 45]

Variations in personal space between ethnic groups are hard to define specifically because of the different ages, socioeconomic levels, and geographical factors involved. It is safe to say that discomfort may arise between people if they are not sensitive to each other's preferred distance for interaction. You've been in a situation where you've wished someone would come closer to you. On other occasions, you may have wished that people wouldn't come so close to you. Sometimes you've probably wanted to come closer to someone else, but weren't sure whether he or she would like it. Distance is language. We have to learn how to communicate with this language more effectively.

TOUCHING

The ultimate closeness to people is in touching them. Lawrence K. Frank describes touching as an important aspect of human development and communication:

The skin is the outer boundary, the envelope which contains the human organism and provides its earliest and most elemental mode of communication.[46]

Ashley Montagu holds a similar position:

. . . adequate tactile satisfaction during infancy and childhood is of fundamental importance for the subsequent healthy behavioral development of the individual.[47]

Montagu refers to touch as:

. . . a sensation to which basic human meanings become attached almost from the moment of birth, is fundamental in the development of human behavior. The raw sensation of touch as stimulus is vitally necessary for the physical survival of the organism. In that sense it may be postulated that the need for tactile stimulation must be added to the repertoire of basic needs in all vertebrates, if not in all invertebrates as well.[48]

Sidney Jourard has conducted research in which he measured various attitudes and experiences of people with regard to touch. Jourard describes some of his early interest in touching:

I watched pairs of people engaged in conversation in coffee shops in San Juan (Puerto Rico), London, Paris, and Gainesville (Florida), counting the number of times that one person touched another at one table during a one-hour sitting. The 'scores' were, for San Juan, 180; for Paris, 110; for London, 0; and for Gainesville, 2. On another occasion I spent two hours walking around the Teaching Hospital at the University of Florida, seeking episodes of body-contact. I watched nurses and physicians tending to patients, I observed relatives in conversation with patients, and I patrolled corridors, watching interchanges between nurses and nurses, physicians and nurses, and physicians with each other. During this time, two nurses' hands touched those of patients to whom they were giving pills; one physician held a patient's wrist as he was taking a pulse; and one intern placed his arm around the waist of a student nurse to whom he was engaged. Clearly, not much physical contact was in evidence. By contrast, I have seen happily married spouses touch one another dozens of times before others—a kiss, a handclasp, a hug. And miserably married persons whom I have seen in psychotherapy have often complained of too little, or too much physical contact. Finally, I have encountered individuals who become furious, and jump as if stung if they are brushed against, or touched on the shoulder or chest during a conversation.[49]

Jourard gave students line drawings of a human body and asked them to indicate where and how often they are touched by their mother, father, same-sex friend, and opposite-sex friend. Females appeared to be more accessible to touch than males. Opposite-sex friends were described by the students as touching them most and fathers were singled out as touching them least. Jourard feels that body contact serves the function of confirming one's bodily being. He suggests that rehabilitation programs in hospitals could be fostered by inclusion of social activities which encourage touching between people.[50]

College students were asked to talk about themselves to another person under one of four conditions. In one condition the listener limited his responding to head nods and expressions of "Yes" and "I see." A second condition was exactly like the first, except that the listener touched the participant briefly just before he or she sat down. Participants in a third condition heard the listener tell something about himself before they talked. A fourth condition was similar to the third, except that the listener also touched the participant. The closer the listener was to the participant in terms of touching and self-disclosure the more open and disclosing the participant was toward him. Both male and female participants said the least about themselves in the first condition and the most about themselves in the fourth condition. Male and female participants were also significantly more favorable toward the listener when he touched them and disclosed himself to them than when he did not.[51]

In a variation of the experiment we read about earlier, female college students secretly left dimes in phone booths in a Boston airport. The students then approached people who "found" the dimes with the following question: "Excuse me. Did you happen to find a dime in this phone booth? I think I might have left one here a few minutes ago." Significantly more dimes were returned if the students came close and touched the person briefly before making the request than if they stood somewhat farther away. In another study, female college students approached people and asked, "Excuse me. Would you lend me a dime?" Significantly more dimes were given when the students touched the people lightly on the arm immediately before making their request.[52]

College students observed videotapes of people they thought were engaged couples. "Engaged" couples who held hands while being interviewed were rated by the students as significantly more close and attentive toward each other and also as more nervous than couples who did not hold hands.[53]

Videotapes were made of job interviews in which a male interviewer either shook hands with the applicant before and after the interview or did not shake hands at all. Job interviewers who shook hands were evaluated by college students as significantly more friendly, warm, sincere, and as liking the job applicant more, as compared with job interviewers who did not shake hands. In addition, job applicants were rated as more friendly, warm, sincere, and better liked by the interviewer when he shook hands with them. It is interesting that a behavior such as touching can influence our perceptions not only of the person who touches, but also of the person who is touched.[54]

As you have seen, most research has found touching to be a positive sign between people. A very different perspective is taken by Nancy Henley. Henley feels that touching can be viewed as a sign of intimacy and solidarity between two people only when it is reciprocal. Instances in which one person touches another and the other (because of propriety or desire) does not touch back, on the other hand, are interpreted by Henley as an expression of interpersonal power. Observations of people in various situations confirmed Henley's hypothesis that higher-status persons (such as bosses, doctors, teachers) more frequently touch lower-status persons (workers, nurses, students) than vice versa. Henley feels that males are given more status in most of society than women and exert this status through the use of unreciprocated touch.

In summary, the findings of more frequent initiation of touching by males may be interpreted as indicative that touching is one of the avenues used by a male-dominated society to keep women in their place, as well as an indication that women's bodies are accessible property. One may be at first appalled to consider that something so human, so natural, as touching, should be perverted into a symbol of status and power. But further reflection reminds us that this is the story of other simple facts of our being, unrelated to status, such as clothing, shelter, and food.

Henley invites men to refrain from using touch as power and women to resist what she calls "the male skin privilege" when it is used to exert control.[55]

I WANT TO HOLD YOUR HAND—OR DO I?

Interpersonal distance is, literally, a touchy matter. As with gaze, the effects of distance on first impressions depend very much on the situation and individuals involved. Coming close to people or touching them can in some cases communicate liking and attraction. At other times close proximity to people can be aversive and disturbing. Watch people around you and see who touches and who doesn't. See if the touching is unilateral or reciprocal. If you haven't made too many enemies (or friends?) yet by gazing at people, you might try touching them.

NOTES

1 THEODORE H. WHITE, *The Making of the President 1960* (New York: Atheneum, 1961). This passage is also quoted by Edward T. Hall in *The Hidden Dimension* (New York: Doubleday, 1969), p. 124.

2 T. BURNS, "Nonverbal Communication," *Discovery*, October 1964, 31–35.

3 R. J. PELLEGRINI, "Some Effects of Seating Position on Social Perception," *Psychological Reports*, 1971, 28, 887–893.

4 F. STRODTBECK and L. HOOK, "The Social Dimensions of a Twelve Man Jury Table," *Sociometry*, 1961, 24, 397–415.

5 D. F. LOTT and R. SOMMER, "Seating Arrangements and Status," *Journal of Personality and Social Psychology*, 1967, 7, 90–94.

6 L. T. HOWELLS and S. W. BECKER, "Seating Arrangement and Leadership Emergence," *Journal of Abnormal and Social Psychology*, 1962, 64, 148–150.

7 R. J. PELLEGRINI, "Some Effects of Seating Position on Social Perception."

8 R. SOMMER, *Personal Space* (Englewood Cliffs, New Jersey: Prentice-Hall, 1969), p. 85.

9 C. HOLAHAN, "Seating Patterns and Patient Behavior in an Experimental Dayroom," *Journal of Abnormal Psychology*, 1972, 80, 115–124.

10 *Ibid.*, p. 122.

11 W. GRIFFITT and R. VEITCH, "Hot and Crowded: Influence of Population Density and Temperature on Interpersonal Affective Behavior," *Journal of Personality and Social Psychology*, 1971, 17, 92–98.

12 A. H. MASLOW and N. L. MINTZ, "Effects of Esthetic Surroundings: I. Initial Effects of Three Esthetic Conditions Upon Perceiving 'Energy' and 'Well-Being' in Faces," *Journal of Psychology*, 1956, 41, 247–254.

13 N. L. MINTZ, "Effects of Esthetic Surroundings: II. Prolonged and Repeated Experience in a 'Beautiful' and 'Ugly' Room," *Journal of Psychology*, 1956, 41, 459–466.

14 C. L. LASSEN, "Effect of Proximity on Anxiety and Communication in the Initial Psychiatric Interview," *Journal of Abnormal Psychology*, 1973, 81, 226–232.

15 M. L. PATTERSON and L. B. SECHREST, "Interpersonal Distance and Impression Formation," *Journal of Personality*, 1970, 38, 161–166.

16 C. L. KLEINKE, R. A. STANESKI, and S. L. PIPP, "Effects of Gaze, Distance, and Attractiveness on Males' First Impressions of Females," *Representative Research in Social Psychology*, 1975, 6, 7–12.

17 M. J. HOROWITZ, "Spatial Behavior and Psychopathology," *The Journal of Nervous and Mental Disease*, 1968, 46, 24–35.

18 M. J. HOROWITZ, D. DUFF, and L. STRATTON, "The Body-Buffer Zone: An Exploration of Personal Space," *Archives of General Psychiatry*, 1964, 11, 651–656.

19 A. KINZEL, "Body-Buffer Zone in Violent Prisoners," *American Journal of Psychiatry*, 1970, 127, 59–64.

20 G. MCBRIDE, M. G. KING, and J. W. JAMES, "Social Proximity Effects on GSR in Human Adults," *Journal of Psychology*, 1965, 61, 153–157.

21 R. SOMMER, *Personal Space*, Chap. 3.

22 M. L. PATTERSON, S. MULLENS, and J. ROMANO, "Compensatory Reactions to Spatial Intrusion," *Sociometry*, 1971, 34, 114–121.

23 M. MEISELS and M. A. DOSEY, "Personal Space, Anger-Arousal, and Psychological Defense," *Journal of Personality*, 1971, 39, 333–344.

24 R. SOMMER, *op. cit.*, p. 28.

25 S. ALBERT and J. M. DABBS, JR., "Physical Distance and Persuasion," *Journal of Personality and Social Psychology*, 1970, 15, 265–270.

26 R. E. KLECK, "Interaction Distance and Non-Verbal Agreeing Responses," *British Journal of Social and Clinical Psychology*, 1970, 9, 180–182.

27 S. MILGRAM, "Some Conditions of Obedience and Disobedience to Authority," *Human Relations*, 1965, 18, 57–76.

28 F. N. WILLIS, "Initial Speaking Distance as a Function of the Speakers' Relationship," *Psychonomic Science*, 1966, 5, 221–222.

29 A. MEHRABIAN, "Inference of Attitude From the Posture, Orientation, and Distance of a Communicator," *Journal of Consulting and Clinical Psychology*, 1968, 32, 296–308.

30 A. MEHRABIAN, "Relationship of Attitude to Seated Posture, Orientation, and Distance," *Journal of Personality and Social Psychology*, 1968, 10, 26–30.

31 A. MEHRABIAN and J. T. FRIAR, "Encoding of Attitude by a Seated Communicator Via Posture and Position Cues," *Journal of Consulting and Clinical Psychology*, 1969, 33, 330–336.

32 A. MEHRABIAN, "Inference of Attitude From the Posture, Orientation, and Distance of a Communicator."

33 H. M. ROSENFELD, "Effect of an Approval Seeking Induction on Interpersonal Proximity," *Psychological Reports*, 1965, 17, 120–122.

34 D. Byrne, C. R. Ervin, and J. Lamberth, "Continuity Between the Experimental Study of Attraction and Real-Life Computer Dating," *Journal of Personality and Social Psychology*, 1970, 16, 157–165.

35 M. G. King, "Structural Balance, Tension, and Segregation in a University Group," *Human Relations*, 1964, 17, 221–225.

36 W. E. Leipold, "Psychological Distance in a Dyadic Interview," Unpublished doctoral dissertation, University of North Dakota, 1963. This research is discussed by R. Sommer in *Personal Space*, p. 30.

37 S. A. Karabenick and M. Meisels, "Effects of Performance Evaluation on Interpersonal Distance," *Journal of Personality*, 1972, 40, 275–286.

38 M. A. Dosey and M. Meisels, "Personal Space and Self-Protection," *Journal of Personality and Social Psychology*, 1969, 11, 93–97.

39 M. G. King, "Interpersonal Relations in Preschool Children and Average Approach Distance," *Journal of Genetic Psychology*, 1966, 109, 109–116.

40 R. Kleck, "Physical Stigma and Nonverbal Cues Emitted in Face-to-Face Interaction," *Human Relations*, 1969, 22, 51–60.

41 R. E. Kleck, P. L. Buck, W. L. Goller, R. S. London, J. R. Pfeiffer, and D. P. Vukcevic, "Effect of Stigmatizing Conditions on the Use of Personal Space," *Psychological Reports*, 1968, 23, 111–118.

42 S. Thayer and L. Alban, "A Field Experiment on the Effect of Political and Cultural Factors on the Use of Personal Space," *Journal of Social Psychology*, 1972, 88, 267–272.

43 J. C. Baxter, "Interpersonal Spacing in Natural Settings," *Sociometry*, 1970, 33, 444–456.

44 J. R. Aiello and S. E. Jones, "Field Study of the Proxemic Behavior of Young School Children in Three Subcultural Groups," *Journal of Personality and Social Psychology*, 1971, 19, 351–356.

45 S. E. Jones and J. R. Aiello, "Proxemic Behavior of Black and White First-, Third- and Fifth-Grade Children," *Journal of Personality and Social Psychology*, 1973, 25, 21–27.

46 L. K. Frank, "Tactile Communication," *Genetic Psychology Monographs*, 1957, 56, 209–255.

47 M. F. A. Montagu, *Touching: The Human Significance of the Skin* (New York: Harper & Row, 1971), p. 334.

48 *Ibid.*, p. 332.

49 S. M. Jourard, "An Exploratory Study of Body-Accessibility," *British Journal of Social and Clinical Psychology*, 1966, 5, 221–231.

50 *Ibid.*

51 S. M. Jourard and R. Friedman, "Experimenter-Subject 'Distance' and Self-Disclosure," *Journal of Personality and Social Psychology*, 1970, 15, 278–282.

52 C. L. Kleinke, "Compliance to Requests Made by Gazing and Touching Experiments in Field Settings," *Journal of Experimental Social Psychology*, in press.

53 C. L. KLEINKE, F. B. MEEKER, and C. LA FONG, "Effects of Gaze, Touch, and Use of Name on Evaluation of 'Engaged' Couples," *Journal of Research in Personality*, 1974, 7, 368–373.

54 R. A. Staneski, C. L. KLEINKE, and F. B. MEEKER, "Evaluation of Job Applicants Who are Touched or Called by Name by Ingratiating and Noningratiating Interviewers," Paper presented at the meeting of the Western Psychological Association, Anaheim, Calif., 1973.

55 N. M. HENLEY, "Power, Sex, and Nonverbal Communication: The Politics of Touch," in P. Brown (Ed.), *Radical Psychology* (New York: Harper & Row, 1974).

4

Body Language

both sides

At a psychology convention in San Diego, Pavel Machotka described research in which participants were asked to look at Renaissance paintings and give their impressions of the people in the paintings. Participants took a long time to study the pictures and paid attention to a wide variety and range of features in the figures and backgrounds. One of the most important cues used to judge the people portrayed in the various works was whether they crossed their arms and legs to close off their body space or opened their arms and legs to give access to their body space. Other important factors were the direction of gaze of the people in a painting, whether they were clothed or nude, how and where they pointed or leaned, whether they were relaxed or tense, and how closely they were grouped together.

One finding in the study that was particularly striking was the relatively negative reaction given—especially by male participants—to Botticelli's *Birth of Venus*. Venus is an attractive woman in the painting, but she stands in such a way as to close off her body from approach. It occurred to Machotka that the way in which Venus was standing may have put the participants off and made them feel angry with her.

In order to test further people's reactions to body posture, a series of figures was drawn of a nude woman standing in a number of different body positions. In one case the woman covered her body with her arms, as in the painting of Venus. In another case the woman in the drawing held her arms in an open embracing position, and in a third case she stood with her arms at her sides. When people rated these drawings they described the first woman as being self-concerned, cold, rejecting, and unyielding. The second woman, with her arms outstretched, was perceived as immodest, dramatic, and exhibitionistic. The woman with her arms at her sides was admired most and judged as being natural, calm, and approachable. When nude, the woman with her arms outstretched apparently appeared to be too open. When viewed in the same posture, but clothed, she was judged as perfectly natural. This was probably because with a dress on, the woman had enough of a body boundary to compensate for the openness of her outstretched arms. We can begin to see how our body postures and positions influence the way people perceive us.

In a second study, Machotka had figures drawn in one of which a man and woman reached out toward each other, in another of which the man reached out toward the woman and the woman leaned away, and in the last of which the woman reached out toward the man and the man leaned away. The man and the woman were both seen as warm, sincere, erotic, active, and aggressive if each reached toward the other, and as cold, calculating, noneerotic, passive, and constrained if they leaned away from each other. A man who reached out toward a woman who leaned away was judged aggressive, active, and evil, while a man who reached out toward a woman who reciprocated was perceived as warm, free, and erotic. A woman reaching out toward a man who leaned away was seen as much more aggressive and action-oriented than a woman who reached out toward a man who reciprocated. A third study found that the perceived power of a man in a drawing could be increased if other people in the drawing focused their gaze toward him rather than away from him. We can also see how the body postures of people around us influence the way we are perceived by others.

A final example used by Machotka to show how the relationship between people's body positions affects how they are judged is a scene from Charlie Chaplin's movie *The Great Dictator*, in which the Hitler and Mussolini figures are in a barbershop. Hitler raises his chair above Mussolini. Mussolini then raises his chair above Hitler. Hitler jacks his seat up more and Mussolini follows. In the end both figures reach the ceiling and fall to the floor.[1]

THE LANGUAGE OF LIKING

Sometimes when we meet people we get an immediate feeling for whether or not they seem to like us. Does this have anything to do with how they are standing or sitting? Does the way in which we are standing or sitting have any effect on how other people perceive us?

Albert Mehrabian has conducted a large program of research to find out how various body postures and positions are related to the amount of liking and attraction between people. In one series of studies, photographs were taken of people sitting in a number of different positions and postures. Participants in the research were then asked to look at the people in the photographs and give whatever impressions they thought they would have if they were to meet the people in real life. The faces of the people in the photographs were covered so that the participants would make their judgments only on the basis of posture, and not on looks or facial expression. Both men and women in the photographs were liked better if they leaned forward rather than back. Leaning forward was somewhat more important for liking of the women in the photographs than it was for liking of the men. Females were better liked if they sat in an open position with their arms and legs uncrossed rather than in a closed position with their arms and legs crossed. These differences in posture did not make as much difference for liking of the men, though there was a slight tendency for participants to prefer men with their arms and legs crossed. Both men and women in the photographs were preferred if they sat with their bodies relaxed rather than tense.[2]

In another series of studies, Mehrabian asked participants to approach a coat-rack pretending it was a person whom they either liked or disliked and who was either of high or low status. Experimenters observed the participants through a one-way mirror and made careful ratings of their postures and body positions. Participants oriented their heads and bodies more directly toward hypothetical persons of high rather than low status. Female participants tended to stand more openly with their arms and legs uncrossed when approaching an imaginary person of high status. Male participants did not differ in body openness toward high or low status persons. Both male and female participants had greater body relaxation when approaching an imaginary person of low status. When approaching an imaginary person of high status they were more tense. Male and female participants tended to cross their arms in front of them when approaching an imaginary person whom they did not like. When approaching an imaginary person whom they did like, participants held their arms more to their sides. When the imaginary person being approached was disliked, male and female participants leaned back with their bodies much more than when the imaginary person was liked.[3,4,5]

A number of different studies have investigated the relationship between body posture and liking when two people are interacting. Female college students were told that they would be introduced to another female student and that they would be left together for a few minutes to get to know each other. Half of the students were instructed to try and get the other girl to like them. The remaining students were given instructions to avoid friendship with the other girl. All of the conversations were observed through a one-way mirror by experimenters who made records of the participants' body movements. Females who were trying to make friends with the other girl gave significantly more smiles and gesticulations during the conversation compared with females who were trying to avoid friendship. Gesticulations were defined as "any noticeable movement of the arm, hand, or finger, not in moving contact with another part of the body." Females seeking friendship also had a slight tendency to nod their heads and scratch or touch themselves more than females avoiding friendship.[6]

Participants in an experiment interacted with an experimenter who leaned toward them and smiled or leaned away from them, did not smile, and drummed his fingers impatiently. The participants perceived the experimenter as being much warmer and they were significantly more influenced by his approval when he leaned forward and smiled than when he did not.[7]

Female college students came into a room in pairs and were given a short lecture by a female experimenter. During the lecture the experimenter turned her body toward one of the students 90 percent of the time and toward the other student 10 percent of the time. Both students later judged that the experimenter had preferred the student toward whom she had turned her body more often.[8]

College students who came to take part in an experiment were brought into a waiting room with another person for two minutes. Experimenters observed their interaction during this time through a one-way mirror and made recordings of their body movements and patterns of talking. The responses recorded were found to fall into certain fairly distinct categories. When people were trying to be affiliative they tended to talk and nod their heads a lot, they had positive facial expressions and tone of voice, and they engaged in a good deal of gesturing with their hands and arms. People who were nervous tended to move their arms or legs a lot and lean away from the other person. People who were seeking closeness or friendship with the other person oriented their body toward the person and maintained a fairly close physical distance.[9,10]

Observational studies of interactions in our culture have suggested that certain body movements are associated with courting behavior between men and women. According to one investigator:

Courtship readiness is most clearly evidenced by a state of high muscle tonus. Sagging disappears, jowling and bagginess around the eyes decreases, the torso becomes more erect, and pot-bellied slumping disappears or decreases. The legs are brought into tighter tonus, a condition seen in "cheese cake" and associated with the professional model or athlete. The eyes seem to be brighter . . . women may stroke their hair, or glance at their makeup in the mirror, or sketchily rearrange their clothing. Men usually comb or stroke their hair, button or readjust their coats, or pull up their socks.[11]

Another group of investigators gave men and women a list describing over one hundred different nonverbal behaviors in which a person could engage while interacting with someone else and asked them to pick out the behaviors that would be interpreted as especially negative and also the behaviors they thought would appear as especially positive. The most negative or cold nonverbal behaviors chosen by the judges were frowning, looking at the ceiling, moving away, giving a yawn, sneering, giving a cold stare, picking one's teeth, shaking one's head negatively, looking away, and cleaning one's fingernails. The most positive or warm nonverbal behaviors were judged to be touching or moving toward the other person, looking at the other person, smiling, nodding one's head affirmatively, using expressive hand gestures, opening the eyes or raising the eyebrows, and orienting one's body toward the other person. To test the effects of these nonverbal behaviors on first impressions, videotapes were made of an actress engaging in various combinations of the behaviors while she was supposedly engaging in a conversation with a man she had just met. Students who observed the taped conversations (thinking they were real) gave significantly more positive evaluations to the female when she engaged in the warm nonverbal behaviors and significantly more negative evaluations when she portrayed the cold nonverbal behaviors.[12]

The studies investigating body language generally conclude that body postures of openness, forward lean, relaxation (except when people are preparing to court and are showing increased attention toward one another), and direct body orientation are related to liking and attraction between people. The only exception would be when someone is just too "open" for the situation and it comes off as inappropriate. People who are seeking friendship with another engage in more head nodding, gesturing, body movement, and smiling than people who are either uninterested in or are avoiding such friendship.

OUR BODIES BETRAY DECEPTION

We often have a pretty good inkling of whether or not someone is telling the truth. How does this come about? In Chapter 2 we learned that people tend to reduce their gaze toward others when they are being dishonest and increase their gaze toward others when trying to be persuasive. Studies have also shown that there are differences in body movements when people are deceitful rather than truthful. A successful con man has learned to minimize the gaze and body cues which might otherwise betray his deception. Most of us have not learned to manipulate our body cues as well as our verbal statements and we often "leak" our true feelings through various body postures and positions. Freud put it this way:

He that has eyes to see and ears to hear may convince himself that no mortal can keep a secret. If his lips are silent, he chatters with his finger tips; betrayal oozes out of him at every pore.[13]

The question of how our bodies betray deception has been studied in several ways. In one experiment, judges were shown silent films of real interviews involving patients who were known to be hiding their true feelings about certain problems they were having. Half of the judges saw only the faces and heads of the patients in the films and half of the judges saw only the bodies of the patients. The judges did not know that the people they were watching were patients and were not told specifically what they should look for. When they were asked to give their impressions of the people in the films, the judges who saw the heads and faces were much more mislead and deceived about the patients' feelings and motivations than the judges who saw only the bodies. One explanation for this result is that we learn in our society to be more aware of our facial expressions than our bodily expressions and therefore do not monitor our bodies as much as our faces when we are trying to be deceptive. The patients in this study were presumably able to conceal their true feelings from their facial expressions but not from their bodily expressions.[14]

Participants in another experiment were asked to give a short speech to another person and either try to be very persuasive toward one position or more or less neutral and objective. The speeches were videotaped and later shown to judges who scored the body movements of the participants on a number of dimensions. The participants were found to engage in higher rates of head nodding and gesticulation, more facial expression, and higher degrees of speech rate, speech volume, intonation, and smoothness of speech when they were trying to be persuasive rather than objective.[15]

Experiments have also been conducted in which participants were asked to give persuasive arguments in favor of issues in which they did not believe and in favor of issues in which they did believe. When the participants were being deceitful and trying to convince an audience of something which they did not believe, they had less frequent body movements, they leaned or turned away from their audience more, they smiled more, and they talked less, more slowly, and had more speech errors.[16,17] It appears that people are more animated in their movements when they believe what they are arguing for and more controlled and contained when they are being deceitful.

THE LANGUAGE OF EMOTION

An obvious way to find out how people are feeling at a given time is to ask them. Another approach, as we will discover later, is to look at their facial expressions. There are also times when we get impressions about other people's emotional states from their postures and body movements. An example of this is shown in a study which found that people could read typed statements made by someone being interviewed and accurately choose which of two photographs of the interviewee was taken at the particular time the statement in the interview was made. The statements in the interview were correctly matched to pictures showing only the interviewee's head as well as to pictures showing only the interviewee's body.[18]

Emotion in Body Movements. Several studies have measured the body movements of people when they either pretended to be or actually were involved in various emotional states. College students in one experiment were given the task of approaching another person either in a neutral state or while attempting to portray the emotions of fear, anger, or sorrow. The students came fairly close to the other person when portraying anger and stayed very far away when portraying fear. Most eye contact was given to the other person in the fear condition and least eye contact was given in the condition of sorrow. When attempting to portray sorrow, the students walked toward the other person fairly quickly. When acting angry, the students approached the other person slowly.[19]

In another study, college students were interviewed and their verbal responses were coded as to whether they fit into categories of overt hostility, covert hostility, or other feelings. Overt hostility included statements in which the students admitted and expressed hostile feelings in themselves. Covert hostility was defined by statements in which students talked about hostility in other persons and in situations that did not directly involve themselves. Careful scoring of the students' body postures during the interview showed that when they were expressing overt hostility they tended to engage mainly in "object-focused" movements, that is, in small gestures used to punctuate and emphasize verbal statements. These do not usually involve touching one's own body. When the students were expressing covert hostility in the interviews their body movements were generally body-focused, such as touching the hands together and touching or rubbing other parts of one's body.[20]

People being interviewed in films were scored for their moods and body movements. Results showed that during periods of anger there were many head and leg movements, but few hand movements. During depressed moods, there were few movements of the head, but many leg movements.[21] Psychiatric patients were observed during interviews with therapists and found to have significantly more body movements and to gesture significantly more when they were under stress and talking about disturbing topics than when they were not stressed and were talking about neutral topics.[22]

It is apparent that body movements can give us clues about negative emotional states of another person. Anger is reflected by approaching someone slowly, but closely, and by head and leg movements. Overt hostility is shown in object-focused movements and covert hostility is expressed by body-focused movements. Depression is accompanied by leg movements and stress results in higher overall body movement. Fear manifests itself in keeping one's distance from another and watching him or her very closely.

Paul Ekman has attempted in some of his research to compare body movements and facial expressions on the basis of what they tell us about emotions.

Participants in Ekman's studies were shown photographs of people that were taken under various emotional conditions in an interview. One-third of the participants saw photographs of the people's bodies only, one-third saw photographs of the people's heads only, and a third group of participants were given complete photographs of the people. It turned out that participants who had only faces to judge were most accurate about what particular emotion (such as happiness, surprise, fear, anger) was being expressed. Participants who saw only bodies had the most agreement about the intensity or strength of the emotions of the people in the photographs. Seeing the faces did not increase the participants' accuracy of judgments of emotional intensity and seeing body postures did not increase the participants' accuracy of judgments of particular emotions being expressed.[23,24]

Emotion in Hand Gestures. A special interest of some investigators of body language has been in finding out how we communicate feelings specifically with hand gestures. In one study, different emotional states were aroused in participants by confronting them with various issues and questions and asking them to respond. The participants' judgments of their feelings at given times and the various hand gestures they were engaging in at that time were recorded and later correlated. Attitudes of affection coincided with holding one or two fingers on one hand with the opposite hand, attitudes of shame correlated with hand-to-nose or hand-to-lips gestures, aggression was related to fist gestures, frustration to an open hand dangling between the legs, and suspicion was correlated with two hands folded at the fingertips or one hand placed over the other.

There were some gestures that were more common for males and some that were more common for females. Males were more likely to hold one hand over the opposite hand or opposite wrist, dangle one hand between their legs, and interlace or fold their fingers together. Females tended more than males to hold one of their hands in a cupped position, to grasp one or two fingers of one hand with the other hand, to sit with their wrists crossed, and to hold one hand to their chin.[25,26]

Two other studies used judgments of photographs to study various hand gestures. Photographs were taken of an actor's hands as he was attempting to portray thirty-five different emotions. These thirty-five photographs were shown to judges who were given the task of guessing which emotion was being portrayed. Seventy-five percent of the judges agreed on the picture in which the actor was expressing worship (clasped hands) and 55 percent agreed on the actor's attempt to portray pleading or begging (open hands with palms up). About one-third of the judges gave similar labels to the photographs in which the actor was portraying thoughtfulness (one hand held loosely over the other), determination (one hand in a fist, the other hand covering it), and bewilderment (hands held with palms facing straight out and fingers spread). One-fourth of the judges agreed on the hand expressions of threat, humility, surprise, sympathy, distrust, and anger. Only 5 percent of the judges agreed on the hand expressions of admiration, scorn, defiance, and disgust. Men and women agreed fairly closely in their judgments. The study was repeated with the actor portraying the thirty-five emotions on film and the results were very similar.[27]

In a more recent study, judges were asked to make ratings of pictures of human hands in a large number of different positions. In general, judges rated hands in a gripping or groping position as active and intentional. Hands in a cupped position were seen by the judges as begging and passive. Hands held so that they hung down in a drooping position were evaluated as weak, submissive, and shy. Hands held so that they pushed or faced outward from the body were rated by judges as immature, uncontrolled, and impulsive.[28]

Films taken of patients in psychiatric interviews were analyzed frame by frame to see what kinds of hand movements were used. The hand movements were then associated with what was going on in the interview at the time they were being used. Throwing the hands in the air and flailing of arms occurred primarily in periods of frustration and anger, often related to periods when the patient expressed feelings of ambivalence about family members. A hand-shrugging movement was associated with expressions of uncertainty, confusion, and inability to cope. Using the hands to cover the eyes occurred primarily during crying and expression of shame. Rubbing the arms of the chair seemed to show restlessness and agitation, but did not correlate with any one topic or issue of conversation. Gesturing with the hand out toward the interviewer occurred mainly in conjunction with an attempt to answer a direct question, often with verbal expressions of "I don't know," "Probably," "I mean," or "I suppose." Further study showed that hand movements of patients changed in many ways between the time they were admitted to hospitalization for psychotherapy and the time they were discharged. Acts of rubbing the chair arms and shrugging with the hands or throwing the hands in the air decreased markedly. Instead, a greater diversity of hand movements was developed that was not so marked with repetitiveness and agitation.[29]

BODY MOVEMENTS AS REGULATORS IN AN INTERACTION

In addition to expressing emotions, body movements can serve as signs or markers to regulate the progress of a conversation between two people. One study in which conversations were carefully observed and recorded showed that people tended to nod their heads most frequently at junctions in their conversation, when one person stopped talking and the other began. The data from this study seemed to indicate that listeners in conversations might nod their heads when they are ready to talk and speakers might nod their heads when they are ready to listen.[30] In a similar study it was found that people who were speaking engaged in more body movements at the very beginning of sentences and immediately after pauses than during the more fluent periods in their speech. The body movements of speakers appeared to result from increased arousal when they were trying to formulate their thoughts and when they were trying to emphasize a certain point.[31]

Albert Scheflen has indicated that we learn to use various head and hand movements during a conversation as markers to communicate when we wish to pause, when we wish to continue talking, and when we are ready to listen. Through careful observations of filmed therapeutic interviews Scheflen found that the sequences of head and hand movements during an interaction are very similar for different individuals and seem to represent a culturally learned method of communication to regulate the progress of an interaction.[32]

Body movements can also be related to the quality or success of a conversation. The body postures of a patient and therapist during a psychotherapy session were scored according to whether they were congruent or noncongruent with each other. A congruent situation existed when the patient and therapist maintained body positions which were either mirror images or identical in configuration. A noncongruent condition was when the patient and therapist sat in postures which did not match or relate in any way. Analysis of the conversation found that the verbal statements of the patient and therapist tended to be positive, interpersonal, specific, and relevant to the therapeutic situation when the body postures of the patient and therapist were congruent. When the patient and therapist were in a noncongruent configuration the conversation was more self-oriented, negational, nonspecific, and self-contradictory.[33]

HOW IS BODY LANGUAGE LEARNED?

We have seen that people's body movements and postures can be influenced by their motives and emotions. We have also learned that our judgments or impressions of people can be influenced by the body movements and postures in which they are engaging at a particular time. Some people we know are very astute at judging the feelings of others. Other people seem to be particularly insensitive to the feelings transmitted by those around them. When we consider the question of whether or not it is possible to measure how accurate various people are in reading body language it becomes apparent that we have to pay strong attention to the group or culture of which they are members. Body postures and movements may have vastly different meanings to people in different cultures. For this reason it is probably not feasible to speak of an *overall* ability and accuracy in interpreting body language. It is conceivable that people can learn to become sensitive to body language within a given culture.

Studies in the United States have shown that men and women differ in the amount of time that they engage in various body postures. Observations taken of men and women in therapeutic interviews found that men pointed more frequently than women and women shrugged their shoulders, shook their heads, and turned their palms up and out more frequently than men. Women folded their arms across their waist more often than men and kept their legs crossed at their knees throughout a large part of the interview. Men did not use the closed-knee leg cross very often. They sat either in an open-leg cross, with one ankle on the knee of the other leg, or with both feet on the floor. It was felt by the experimenters who conducted the study that the men's pointing behaviors and open-leg behaviors represented an active or intrusive pattern, while females, with their folded-arm posture and predominantly closed-leg cross, were seen as being more inhibited or inclusive.[34]

There are also variations in the use of body language within various subcultures of the United States. Nursery-school children from varying backgrounds were asked to pretend that they were in a situation in which they were trying to tell something to somebody else without talking. The children were told that they could use their hands, arms, or fingertips, or any other part of their body to get the message across. The messages that the children were asked to communicate were "Go away," "Come here," "Yes," "No," "Be quiet," "How many," "How big," "What shape," "I don't know," "Good-bye," "Hi," and "Attention-seeking." Two adult observers behind a one-way mirror scored the children to see how accurately they could transmit the various messages. It was found that middle-class children were more accurate in transmitting the messages than lower-class children and that children with one year of school did better than children with no school experience. The same differences in accuracy were found when the children were asked to pick out the meaning of the various messages that were transmitted by an adult.[35] But because the adult observers used in the study were from the middle class, it is not necessarily true that children from lower socioeconomic groups were really less accurate in communicating nonverbal messages. Presumably, adults from lower socioeconomic groups would have the same difficulties in understanding the nonverbal messages transmitted by middle-class children and in communicating nonverbal messages to them. The importance of this study is that it shows how people from various groups may have trouble in understanding one another's body language.

In Chapter 3 we discussed the misunderstandings that can arise between members of different cultures because of variations in the ways they use personal space. In their book *The Ugly American*, Lederer and Burdick give a rather powerful description of how lack of sensitivity to other cultures can lead to discomfort and animosity. There are also differences between cultures in the use of body language that must be understood before accurate communication can occur. Some of these differences are described in a very interesting article by Weston LaBarre:

> The Semang, pygmy Negroes of interior Malaya, thrust the head sharply forward for "yes" and cast the eyes down for "no." The Abyssinians say "no" by jerking the head to the right shoulder, and "yes" by throwing the head back and raising the eyebrows. The Dyaks of Borneo raise their eyebrows to mean "yes" and contract them slightly to mean "no." The Maori say "yes" by raising the head and chin; the Sicilians say "no" in exactly the same manner.
>
> Hissing in Japan is a polite deference to social superiors; the Basuto applaud by hissing, but in England hissing is rude and public disapprobation of an actor or a speaker. Spitting in many parts of the world is a sign of utmost contempt; and yet among the Masai of Africa it is a sign of affection and benediction.
>
> Western man stands up in the presence of a superior; the Fijians and the Tongans sit down. In some contexts we put on more clothes as a sign of respect; the Friendly Islanders take them off. The Toda of South India raise the open right hand to the face, with the thumb on the bridge of the nose, to express respect; a gesture almost identical among Europeans is an obscene expression of extreme disrespect.

LaBarre states that anthropologists should attempt to become sensitive to the body languages in cultures they visit in order to save embarrassment and possibly their lives.[36]

Because gestures and body postures can mean different things to different people in different places, we should be cautious about playing the popular game of pointing out a special meaning for every eye blink or movement a person makes. On the other hand, it would be valuable for us to attempt to learn how body movements coincide with various feelings and attitudes that we have and that are shared by people around us. In order to become more sensitive to body language we have to get feedback on how accurate our interpretations and impressions are. Actors often use the technique of placing themselves in various emotional states and concentrating on what is happening to every aspect of their bodies during each experience. In this way, a more intimate communication between one's body and one's feelings can be developed. Professional dancers, because of their training, are very sensitive to bodily information.[37]

An increased understanding for other people through their body language can be gained if we are careful to get confirmation of our first impressions from them and avoid making judgments and generalizations on the basis of those impressions alone.

NOTES

1 P. MACHOTKA, "Body Movement As Communication," *Dialogues: Behavioral Science Research* (Boulder, Colorado: Western Interstate Commission for Higher Education, 1965), pp. 33–65.

2 A. MEHRABIAN, "Inference of Attitudes from the Posture, Orientation, and Distance of a Communicator," *Journal of Consulting and Clinical Psychology*, 1968, 32, 296–308.

3 *Ibid.*

4 A. MEHRABIAN, "Relationship of Attitude to Seated Posture, Orientation, and Distance," *Journal of Personality and Social Psychology*, 1968, 10, 26–30.

5 A. MEHRABIAN and J. T. FRIAR, "Encoding of Attitude by a Seated Communicator Via Posture and Position Cues," *Journal of Consulting and Clinical Psychology*, 1969, 33, 330–336.

6 H. M. ROSENFELD, "Approval-Seeking and Approval-Avoiding Functions of Verbal and Nonverbal Responses in the Dyad," *Journal of Personality and Social Psychology*, 1966, 4, 597–605.

7 M. REECE and R. WHITMAN, "Expressive Movements, Warmth, and Verbal Reinforcement," *Journal of Abnormal and Social Psychology*, 1962, 64, 234–236.

8 A. MEHRABIAN, "Orientation Behaviors and Nonverbal Attitude Communication," *Journal of Communication*, 1967, 17, 324–332.

9 A. MEHRABIAN, "Verbal and Nonverbal Interaction of Strangers in a Waiting Situation," *Journal of Experimental Research in Personality*, 1971, 5, 127–138.

10 A. MEHRABIAN, "Nonverbal Communication," *Nebraska Symposium on Motivation* (University of Nebraska Press, 1971), pp. 107–161.

11 A. E. SCHEFLEN, "Quasi-Courtship Behavior in Psychotherapy," *Psychiatry*, 1965, 28, 245–257.

12 J. CLORE, N. WIGGINS, and S. ITKIN, "Judging Attraction From Nonverbal Behavior: The Gain Phenomenon," *Journal of Personality and Social Psychology*, 1975, in press.

13 S. FREUD, "Fragment of an Analysis of a Case of Hysteria (1905)," *Collected Papers*, Vol. 3 (New York: Basic Books, 1959). This quotation is also cited by P. Ekman and W. V. Friesen in "Nonverbal Leakage and Clues to Deception," *Psychiatry*, 1969, 32, 88–106.

14 P. EKMAN and W. V. FRIESEN, "Nonverbal Leakage and Clues to Deception."

15 A. MEHRABIAN and M. WILLIAMS, "Nonverbal Concomitants of Perceived and Intended Persuasiveness," *Journal of Personality and Social Psychology*, 1969, 13, 37–58.

16 A. MEHRABIAN, "Nonverbal Betrayal of Feeling," *Journal of Experimental Research in Personality*, 1971, 5, 64–73.

17 A. MEHRABIAN, "Nonverbal Communication."

18 P. Ekman, "Body Position, Facial Expression, and Verbal Behavior During Interviews," *Journal of Abnormal and Social Psychology*, 1964, 68, 295–301.

19 D. K. FROMME and C. K. SCHMIDT, "Affective Role Enactment and Expressive Behavior," *Journal of Personality and Social Psychology*, 1972, 24, 413–419.

20 N. FREEDMAN, T. BLASS, A. RIFKIN, and F. QUITKIN, "Body Movements and the Verbal Encoding of Aggressive Affect," *Journal of Personality and Social Psychology*, 1973, 26, 72–85.

21 A. T. DITTMANN, "The Relationship Between Body Movements and Moods in Interviews," *Journal of Consulting Psychology*, 1956, 20, 480.

22 P. SAINESBURY, "Gestural Movement During Psychiatric Interviews," *Psychosomatic Medicine*, 1955, 17, 458–469.

23 P. EKMAN, "Differential Communication of Affect by Head and Body Cues," *Journal of Personality and Social Psychology*, 1965, 2, 726–735.

24 P. EKMAN AND W. V. FRIESEN, "Head and Body Cues in the Judgment of Emotion: A Reformulation," *Perceptual and Motor Skills*, 1967, 24, 711–724.

25 M. KROUT, "An Experimental Attempt to Determine the Significance of Unconscious Manual Symbolic Movements," *Journal of General Psychology*, 1954, 51, 121–152.

26 M. KROUT, "An Experimental Attempt to Produce Unconscious Manual Symbolic Movements," *Journal of General Psychology*, 1954, 51, 93–120.

27 L. CARMICHAEL, S. ROBERTS, and N. WESSELL, "A Study of the Judgment of Manual Expression as Presented in Still and Motion Pictures," *Journal of Social Psychology*, 1937, 8, 115–142.

28 S. G. WATSON, "Judgment of Emotion from Facial and Contextual Cue Combinations," *Journal of Personality and Social Psychology*, 1972, 24, 334–342.

29 P. EKMAN and W. V. FRIESEN, "Nonverbal Behavior in Psychotherapy Research," in J. M. Shlein (Ed.), *Research in Psychotherapy*, Vol. 3 (Washington, D.C.: American Psychological Association, 1968), pp. 179–216.

30 A. T. DITTMANN and L. G. LLEWELLYN, "Relationship Between Vocalizations and Head Nods as Listener Responses," *Journal of Personality and Social Psychology*, 1968, 9, 79–84.

31 A. T. DITTMANN and L. G. LLEWELLYN, "Body Movement and Speech Rhythm in Social Conversation," *Journal of Personality and Social Psychology*, 1969, 11, 98–106.

32 A. E. SCHEFLEN, "The Significance of Posture in Communicative Systems," *Psychiatry*, 1964, 27, 316–331.

33 E. J. CHARNEY, "Postural Configurations in Psychotherapy," *Psychosomatic Medicine*, 1966, 28, 305–315.

34 G. F. MAHL, "Gestures and Body Movements in Interviews," in J. M. SHLIEN (Ed.), *Research in Psychotherapy*, Vol. 3 (Washington, D.C.: American Psychological Association, 1968), pp. 295–321.

35 G. MICHAEL and F. N. WILLIS, JR., "The Development of Gestures as a Function of Social Class, Education, and Sex," *Psychological Record*, 1968, 18, 515–519.

36 W. LABARRE, "The Cultural Basis of Emotions and Gestures," *Journal of Personality*, 1947, 16, 49–68.

37 A. T. DITTMANN, M. B. PARLOFF, and D. S. BOOMER, "Facial and Bodily Expressions: A Study of Receptivity of Emotional Cues," *Psychiatry*, 1965, 28, 239–244.

5

Your Face Is a Book

In Chapter 1 we learned that the human face has a pervasive influence on the formation of first impressions, purely on the basis of how beautiful or attractive it is. If we consider, now, the influence of facial *expressions* on first impressions, we enter a whole new dimension of human interaction which affects us in our daily encounters with other people.

Writers throughout the ages have been aware of the richness of messages communicated by the human face. There is some disagreement about whether the messages of the face are reliable or deceptive, but facial expressions do appear, in either case, to be highly influential. Here are some interpretations:[1]

The face is the image of the soul, and the eyes are its interpreter.—*Cicero*

From a man's face I read his character.—*Petronius*

Your face doth testify what you are inwardly.—*Lewis Evans*

The face is oftentimes a true index of the heart.—*James Howell*

In the face the judicious eyes may find the symptoms of a good or evil mind.—*Edward Ward*

Man is read in his face.—*Ben Jonson*

Man is to man the subject of deceit; and that old saying is untrue, "the face is index of the heart."—*R. C.*, TIMES WHISTLE

Men's faces are not to be trusted.—*Juvenal*

When observational studies of a phenomenon such as facial expression become clouded in subjectivity, investigators turn to the more objective methods of scientific research. In a moment we will read about scientific studies that have been conducted on the human face. First, let us consider a bit of the history behind the scientific study of facial expressions.

Charles Darwin took an early interest in facial expressions of men and animals and felt that the existence and influence of facial expressions could be explained by his theory of evolution. Darwin believed that facial movements or expressions were acquired because they served an adaptive function of regulating peaceful interaction. When man developed other forms of communication, facial expressions became less critical for survival, but still remained as an innate form of expressing various feelings and emotions.[2] Most scientists now believe that facial expressions have taken on slightly different meanings in various cultures throughout the world. Later in this chapter we will explore studies that have investigated facial expressions among a variety of cultures to find out which ones are seen as having the same meaning and which ones are not. Our focus will be on facial expressions in humans. We will not concern ourselves with the varieties of expressions in other animals. The questions of how Lassie communicates and whether Davy Crockett really outgrinned that bear will have to be left to other sources.[3]

THE STUDY OF FACIAL EXPRESSIONS

The basic method of studying facial expressions in a scientific manner is to present people with faces expressing different emotions and have them make judgments about what they see. The judgments of various people for the different faces are compared to find out whether or not they agree and to determine what kinds of generalizations and conclusions may be made. Three possible ways of presenting faces to people are through the use of photographs, motion pictures or videotapes, and faces in real life. Having people judge faces in real life would seem to be the most desirable approach, but there are several problems with this method. In order for a study to be sufficiently objective, several people have to judge the same facial expression so that it can be determined if there is any agreement between them. It is also desirable to have permanent records of facial expressions so that results from different studies can be compared with one another at a later time. Another problem is that when live people are used in studies of facial expression there are other variables, such as tone of voice, body posture and movement, and embarrassment, which might tend to interfere with the specific facial judgments that are to be made. Photographs provide a much more objective and controlled method of study, but they show facial expressions only at a particular moment and do not communicate the changes or flow in facial expressions over time.

WHAT CAN WE LEARN FROM FACIAL EXPRESSIONS?

Specific Emotions. Paul Ekman, Wallace Friesen, and Phoebe Ellsworth summarize five studies conducted over a period of thirty years that attempted to separate the various emotions we judge from human faces. The general technique of all these studies was to show people photographs (one study used live faces) expressing a wide variety of emotions and ask the people to provide a label for each specific emotion being shown. The following emotions could be agreed upon by different judges in a fairly consistent manner: happiness, surprise, fear, sadness, anger, disgust/contempt, interest.

There were some limitations to these studies because they used only a small sample of faces in expressing the emotions, the facial expressions had been posed, and the people making the judgments had to match each face to categories of emotions on a list rather than make up their own words. But the fact that the five studies were conducted under a wide range of circumstances and over a long period of time, yet still had comparable results, suggests that the list of seven emotions which were related to facial expressions is fairly reliable.[4]

Dimensions of Emotion. Another way to study what we learn from the human face is to consider facial expressions in terms of dimensions, rather than specific categories, of emotions. Ekman, Friesen, and Ellsworth discuss six investigations carried out during a fifteen-year period that outlined the broad kinds of feelings people can pick out from various facial expressions. Participants in these studies were given the task of looking at faces with different expressions and providing ratings on the dimensions of emotions they thought were being expressed. Everybody felt it possible to evaluate different facial expressions on the basis of how pleasant or unpleasant they appeared to be. There was less agreement on what other dimensions people thought they could judge, but two other possibilities were the amount of attentiveness and the degree of intensity being expressed in a particular facial expression. The studies of dimensions of facial expressions have many of the same weaknesses as the studies of categories of facial expressions. There was generally not a wide variety of faces used, the expressions were posed, and the people making the judgments were limited by a list of dimensions from which they had to choose. Again, though, the fact that the above three dimensions of emotion were found consistently in facial expressions in many different studies would make them appear to be fairly reliable.[5]

HOW ACCURATELY CAN WE JUDGE FACIAL EXPRESSIONS?

Posed Facial Expressions. A fairly straightforward method of measuring how accurately people can interpret facial expressions is to have them look at faces of other people who are portraying various emotions and see if they can correctly judge which emotions they are intended to be. This method does not separate the skill of the people who are portraying the emotions from the accuracy of the judges interpreting the emotions, but the people portraying the emotions are usually trained in such a way that the facial expressions they make are reasonably well standardized. Ekman, Friesen, and Carlsmith draw several conclusions from nine studies of accuracy in interpreting facial expressions that were conducted over a period of thirty years. Some of the studies had judges look at various facial expressions in photographs. Other studies used motion picture films of facial expressions or real-life portrayals. The accuracy of the judges in interpreting the various emotions varied from study to study depending on the different procedures used. For facial expressions of happiness, accuracy of judges ranged from 55 to 100 percent. For surprise, accuracy ranged from 38 to 86 percent; for fear, 16 to 93 percent; anger, 31 to 92 percent; sadness, 19 to 88 percent, disgust/contempt, 41 to 91 percent. Judgments of live facial expressions tended to be somewhat less accurate than judgments of photographs, possibly because other factors such as dress, color of hair or eyes, and body movement may make live judgments more confusing. In any case, the agreement on facial expressions of emotion was far better than chance and indicated that the emotions listed above could be judged in a fairly reliable manner.[6]

Faces in Candid Photographs. Another method of studying accuracy in judging facial expressions is to show judges faces of people in photographs taken in real-life situations. The photographs used in these studies were generally taken from popular magazines. Analysis of the contexts of the photographs (without looking at the faces) gave some notion of what kinds of emotions would be present. Some examples of pictures used included the following: a girl running into the ocean, a baseball fan cheering, a girl in a sock race, a man in a shower with the water unexpectedly turned on, a girl running from a ghost, and a man with his hand stretched toward a hostile crowd. Judges were shown only the faces of the people in the photographs and their interpretations of the emotions in the faces were matched with the emotion manifest in the context of the photograph. In three different studies, judgments of happiness, surprise, fear, and sadness from faces agreed with about 70 percent of the same judgments made from contexts. Emotions of anger and disgust/contempt were less easy to judge, but there were not enough examples of these to get a conclusive sample. Because most of the photographs used in these studies were taken of selected people under unusual circumstances they constitute only a limited sample of faces and emotional expressions in the world around us. In addition, the judgments of what emotions should be expected from the contexts of the photographs are every bit as subjective as the judgments of the facial expressions themselves. But the fact that independent judges had fairly close agreement on what emotions were present when they considered either the context or the facial expression in a photograph suggests that there is a common language of facial expressions, at least for people within the same culture.[7]

Spontaneous Facial Expressions. A third approach to the study of accuracy in interpreting facial expressions is to show people facial expressions captured in various situations and see if they can match the faces with the situations. It has been proven, for example, that people can accurately discriminate photographs and films of faces that were taken during stressful and nonstressful parts of an interview. Judges have also been able to tell the difference between pictures of faces taken of psychiatric patients when they were first admitted to a hospital with disturbed feelings and when they were better adjusted and ready to be discharged.[8]

In a slightly different kind of study, participants were brought into a laboratory and taught that every time a red light came on they would be shocked and every time a green light came on they would not be shocked. During these learning trials the participants were photographed on videotape without their knowledge. In a second phase of the experiment participants were shown portions of videotapes taken of other people in the experiment and required to judge whether the portion was taken during a red-light period or a green-light period. If the judges were wrong they received a shock and if they were correct they avoided a shock. On the whole the judges were able to tell fairly accurately whether a particular videotape portion was taken of somebody who was expecting to receive shock or expecting to avoid shock. Participants who were especially anxious when they were being shocked during the first phase of the experiment were the best judges of others later, but they themselves were the most difficult for others to judge. Interestingly enough, the reason for this seems to be because people who have high internal emotional arousal engage in less external bodily activity. One explanation for the inverse relationship between internal arousal and external behavior is that people who are highly aroused have learned to inhibit or hide this arousal because it is reacted to in a negative manner by others around them. Because the videotapes were taken from the waist up, it is not known to what degree the participants based their judgments on facial cues as opposed to bodily cues. The experiment did show that we can make interpretations about people's emotional states by observing their bodily and facial behaviors.[9]

Another experiment took two participants at a time and made one of them into a sender and one of them into an observer. The sender looked at a number of different kinds of slides and during each slide tried to talk about his or her reactions to it. The observer watched the sender's face through a soundless closed-circuit television system and tried to guess from a list of categories which slide the sender was looking at and whether the sender liked it or not. In order to make sure that the senders were acting in a fairly normal manner they were not told that there was a television camera in the room and that the observer would be watching them. It turned out that female observers were able to judge what kind of slide a sender was viewing but that male observers were not. Because female observers always had female senders and male observers always had male senders it is not known whether females are better senders or better observers. Both male and female observers could accurately interpret whether or not the senders liked or disliked the slides they were looking at. In a manner very similar to that of the previous experiment, senders who were the most emotionally aroused tended to have the hardest facial expressions for observers to judge.[10]

WHAT DO DIFFERENT PARTS OF THE FACE TELL US?

We have seen many examples of the kinds of information that we can learn about other people from their facial expressions. Up to now we have considered facial expressions as a whole and haven't asked specifically if different parts of the face influence us in different ways. Do we learn about peoples' feelings from expressions in their eyes, from their mouth, from the wrinkle of their brow? Or do we learn some things from some parts of the face and different things from other parts of the face? A study conducted in the 1920's to get some information on this question is interesting because of the methods that were used to obtain photographs of faces with different emotions. To get pictures of startled faces, a pistol was fired unexpectedly behind a person's head immediately before a photograph was taken. For facial expressions of pain, a person's finger was forcibly bent backwards immediately before the photograph was taken. Disgust was aroused by presenting the odor of decayed rat tissue, mirth and amusement were evoked by funny stories or jokes, and grief was brought about by hypnotizing the person and suggesting that several members of his family had been killed in a wreck! The photographs obtained were then cut in half across the bridge of the person's nose and put together in various combinations. Judges could then be asked to look at these composite pictures and specify which emotion they thought was present. It turned out that most judges based their ratings of emotions on the bottom half of the faces rather than the top half.[11] A number of other studies have used similar methods to compare the information that we gain from the top and bottom halves of the face. This kind of study has problems, however, because it assumes that what happens to the top half of our face is independent of what happens to the bottom half, and this is probably not the case.[12]

A more fruitful method of study has been to describe which kinds of movements in various parts of the face go along with different emotions. Paul Ekman attempted to do this by taking photographs of faces with different emotions and having judges look at only the eyebrows and forehead, only the eyes and eyelids, or only the lower face from the bridge of the nose down, and then make detailed descriptions of these facial components. The following facial components were found to be present in the six emotions which have been generally studied:[13]

Surprise. Raised curved eyebrows, long horizontal forehead wrinkles. Wide-opened eyes. Dropped-open mouth, lips parted with no stretch or tension.

Fear. Raised and drawn-together brows, short horizontal or vertical forehead wrinkles. Eyes opened, tension in lower lids. Mouth corners drawn back, lips stretched, mouth may or may not be open.

Anger. Brows pulled down, sometimes curved forehead wrinkles centered above the eyes. Upper eyelids appear lowered, lower eyelids tensed and raised, squinting. Lips tightly pressed together or open, squared mouth.

{ **Disgust.** Brows drawn down but not together, wrinkles on bridge of nose. Lower eyelids pushed up and raised, but not tensed. Deep creases from wrinkled nose, mouth open with upper lips raised and lower lip forward, or mouth closed with upper lip pushed up by raised lower lip.

{ **Sadness.** Brows drawn together with inner corners raised and outer corners lowered or level, or brows drawn down in the middle and slightly raised at inner corners. Eyes either glazed, with drooping upper lids and lax lower lids, or upper lids tense and pulled up at inner corner, down at outer corner. Mouth either open with partially stretched trembling lips, or closed with outer corners pulled slightly down.

{ **Happiness.** No distinctive brow-forehead appearance. Eyes may be relaxed or neutral in appearance, or lower lids may be pushed up by lower face action, bagging the lower lids and causing eyes to be narrowed. Outer corners of lips raised, usually also drawn back.

A somewhat broader outline of facial features has been made by a group of investigators who related different expressions of the face to general dimensions of emotion rather than to specific categories. Judges scored photographs of faces on the dimensions of emotion being expressed and then analyzed characteristics of the faces to see which characteristics went along with which dimensions. The following relationships were found:[14]

Pleasantness. Smiling and laughter.

Naturalness. Lack of tension, relaxation in face.

Intensity. Expressiveness, muscular activity in face. Mouth open.

Attention. Muscular activity in face, eyes open.

The various facial measures described in this chapter provide a more detailed understanding of how different parts of the face affect us in different ways. These measures should be of help to us later when we look into whether people from different cultures share common facial expressions and whether they place the same emphasis on specific features of the face that we do.

HOW THE SITUATION INFLUENCES
PERCEPTIONS OF FACIAL EXPRESSIONS

Our perceptions of facial expressions in everyday life are different from our perceptions of photographs or films in a laboratory because of all the other factors of context and situation that are involved. One study measured the importance of context in the perception of faces by showing people a smiling face looking at either a glum face or a frowning face. When the smiling face was looking at the glum face it was rated as dominant, vicious, gloating, and taunting. When the same smiling face was looking at a frowning face it was perceived as peaceful, friendly, and happy. A glum face was seen as angry, jealous, unhappy, and dismayed when paired with a smiling face and aloof, independent, domineering, unafraid, and cool when paired with a frowning face.[15] Other studies have shown that photographs or films of facial expressions are perceived differently if people who look at them are told different stories about what was going on when the pictures were taken. An interesting way to test the relative influence of facial expressions and context on people's judgments is to show them pictures of faces and tell them they were taken in situations that do not agree with the expressions in the faces. For instance, a happy face could be described as having been photographed when the person was in a sad situation. An angry face could be associated with a friendly situation. When studies of this kind are done it is generally found that people making the judgments rely more on the facial expression of the person in the photograph than on the situation in which the person was supposedly involved. There are several factors that affect the results of these studies, including the clarity of the expressions in the faces and the clarity and believability of the supposed situation in which the pictures were taken. Also, varying the context of the facial expressions by telling stories about what was going on when the pictures were taken might not be as strong as varying what is going on in the pictures themselves. The studies that have been done suggest that people's faces communicate things about them that are independent of where they are and what they are doing in a given situation.[16,17,18]

FACIAL EXPRESSIONS IN DIFFERENT CULTURES

In Chapters 3 and 4 we saw examples of how people in various cultures differ in the ways they use and interpret personal space and body language. When different cultures have been compared with regard to facial expressions, however, they have been found to be remarkably similar. Three studies have been conducted in which people in thirteen different countries (U.S., Mexico, England, Germany, France, Brazil, Chile, Africa, Sweden, Greece, Japan, Switzerland, Argentina) were shown photographs (usually of Americans) with various facial expressions and asked to judge in their language which emotion was being expressed. In all countries the judgments for emotions of happiness, fear, surprise, anger, disgust/contempt, and sadness were far more accurate than would be expected by chance. Agreement on happiness was highest, averaging over 90 percent. Agreement on sadness was lowest, ranging from 32 to 90 percent. The Africans had the hardest time judging emotions in American faces. Considering the problems involved in language translation, it appears that facial expressions for the above six emotions have wide cultural generality, but part of the reason why people in the thirteen countries studied had such high agreement on facial expressions for emotion might be because they have had contact with one another and with Americans through movies, travel, magazines, and books.

To investigate still further the universality of human facial expressions, studies were made of people in two preliterate cultures, Borneo and New Guinea. The people chosen in these countries had had little or no previous contact with Western culture. The studies involved telling people in these countries different stories, each involving one emotion, and having them choose from pictures of Americans with various facial expressions the one that corresponded to the emotion in the story. For both adults and children the recognition of emotions was far above chance, ranging from 70 to 90 percent. The easiest facial expression to judge was happiness. Most errors came in trying to distinguish expressions of fear from expressions of surprise. A second part of the study had people in New Guinea listen to stories with various emotions and show how their face would appear if they were in the story. These posed facial expressions were videotaped and later shown to students in the United States. American students were able to judge the emotions in the videotapes with an accuracy well above chance. The easiest emotions for the Americans to identify were happiness and sadness. The most difficult emotions were surprise and fear.

An investigation of spontaneous facial expression was conducted by showing people in the U.S. and Japan a movie and taking a videotape of their facial behavior as they were reacting to the various scenes. In order to get a realistic sample, the people were not told they were being videotaped until after the movie was over. It was felt that Japan and the United States were sufficiently different that if any major cultural variations in facial language existed they would be found by comparing people from these two countries. Four different kinds of scoring were used for the videotaped facial expressions: brows and forehad only, eyes and eyelids only, lower face only, and total face. Comparisons of these scores for the Americans and Japanese showed very close similarity. Japanese and Americans had basically the same kinds of facial expressions as they were watching the movie. As mentioned earlier, the videotapes used in this study were taken without the participants' knowledge. It is interesting that when Japanese are interviewed, they hide their facial expressions or make them appear unduly positive. Americans in interviews are more likely to show negative as well as positive expressions. The evidence from the above studies indicates that there is a nearly universal language of facial expressions. Cultures may differ, however, in how much people are willing to actually show their true emotions.[19,20]

HOW CHILDREN LEARN FACIAL EXPRESSIONS

Research showing that facial expressions of emotion have wide cultural generality has been concerned mainly with the perceptions and expressions of adults. Let us look now at some of the studies of facial expressions conducted in our culture with children. We will learn of some interesting findings that have practical relevance and help us to understand how children's interpretations of facial expressions are developed. Daphne Bugental has conducted a series of studies investigating how children react to facial expressions of their parents and other adults. In one study a series of videotapes was prepared in which a male or female adult acted out a short message. For each message it was arranged that the content, the actor's tone of voice, and the actor's facial expression were either positive or negative. Different combinations of videotaped messages were then shown to judges who were asked to give an evaluation of how friendly or unfriendly the adult in the videotape appeared to be. The judges were either children between the ages of five and twelve years, or adults. The main purpose of the study was to see how the judges would interpret messages that gave contradictory information. An example might be a positive face and tone of voice combined with a negative message, or a positive message and tone of voice combined with a negative face. One particularly striking result was that when the message senders gave a message that was negative in content and tone of voice, if they smiled the adult judges took the message with a grain of salt. Adults have apparently learned that a smile is a sufficient indication that maybe the negative message sender is kidding and doesn't really mean what is being said. Children, on the other hand, took the negative messages very seriously and did not interpret the accompanying smiles as being friendly at all. The tendency of children to assume the worst from conflicting cues was greatest when the message sender was a woman. The implications of this study are important because they suggest that adults may be quite mistaken when they attempt to reduce the impact of a critical statement to a child by smiling.[21]

A second study was conducted by Bugental in which videotapes were made of parents as they interacted with their children. An analysis correlating the kinds of things parents said with whether or not they were smiling led to a surprising conclusion. Fathers tended to smile more when they were saying positive things to their children and smile less when they were saying negative things. This was not the case for mothers. Whether or not a mother smiled had no relationship to the tone or content of what she was saying. It was suggested that women in our society may be conditioned to smile in negative as well as positive situations in order to present a favorably submissive feminine appearance. If women's smiles are independent of their true feelings it is not surprising that children in the previous study did not rely on the facial expressions of women in their judgments of the messages. Apparently children have learned that a woman's smile may not reflect her true feelings, but they do not yet understand the subtlety of the smile as a means of kidding or joking.[22]

When the tendencies of mothers to hide their true feelings becomes too extreme some real problems can result. A study comparing families with disturbed children and families with normal children found that mothers of disturbed children had a much greater likelihood of sending messages with contradictory meaning than mothers of normal children. There was no such trend for fathers. A conflicting message sent by mothers of disturbed children typically contained a critical or disapproving statement spoken in a positive "syrupy" voice or with a smiling facial expression. By sending this kind of message the mother is putting the child into what is often called a double bind. The child who takes the message literally and assumes that the mother is angry suffers because the mother insists that she is not angry. The child who assumes that the mother's smile means that she is not angry suffers because chances are that the mother really is angry. When children are frustrated by such a denial of true feelings in the home it is not surprising that they end up acting out in the neighborhood and in school.[23]

THE RICHNESS OF THE HUMAN FACE

Artists, photographers, and directors of movies and plays are well aware of the richness of messages communicated by the human face. Mimes like Marcel Marceau have devoted their lives to understanding and becoming sensitive to the intricacies of facial expression. A wealth of information and beauty is waiting for us if we take the time to notice people more carefully. At the beginning of this chapter we read examples of how facial expressions have been perceived by people over time. Paul Ekman, one of the most important contemporary researchers in the area, has expressed the following feelings about the human face:[24]

The human face—in repose and in movement, at the moment of death as in life, in silence and in speech, when alone and with others, when seen or sensed from within, in actuality or as represented in art or recorded by the camera—is a commanding, complicated, and at times confusing source of information. The face is *commanding* because of its very visibility and omnipresence. While sounds and speech are intermittent, the face even in repose can be informative. And, except by veils or masks, the face cannot be hidden from view. There is no facial maneuver equivalent to putting one's hands in one's pockets. Further, the face is the location for sensory inputs, life-necessary intake, and communicative output. The face is the site for the sense receptors of taste, smell, sight, and hearing, the intake organs for food, water, and air, and the output location for speech. The face is also commanding because of its role in early development; it is prior to language in the communication between parent and child.

NOTES

1 B. STEVENSON (Ed.), *The Macmillan Book of Proverbs, Maxims, and Famous Phrases* (New York: The Macmillan Company, 1948), pp. 738–739.
2 C. DARWIN, *The Expression of Emotions in Man and Animals* (London: John Murray, 1872). This issue is also discussed by P. Ekman, "Facial Expressions of Emotion," *Nebraska Symposium on Motivation* (Lincoln: University of Nebraska Press, 1971), pp. 207–283.
3 Facial communication in animals has been discussed by I. Vine, "Communication by Facial-Visual Signals: A Review and Analysis of Their Role in Face-to-Face Encounters," in J. H. Crook (Ed.), *Social Behavior in Animals and Man* (London and New York: Academic Press, 1969).
4 P. EKMAN, W. V. FRIESEN, AND P. ELLSWORTH, *Emotion in the Human Face* (New York: Pergamon Press, 1972). Much of the organization and data in this

chapter are based on this book. I recommend it highly to the reader who is interested in studying research on the human face in more detail.

5 P. EKMAN, W. V. FRIESEN, AND P. ELLSWORTH, Chapter 14.

6 *Ibid.,* Chapter 15, Part E.

7 *Ibid.,* Chapter 15, Part C.

8 *Ibid.,* Chapter 15, Part D.

9 J. T. LANZETTA AND R. E. KLECK, "Encoding and Decoding of Nonverbal Affect in Humans," *Journal of Personality and Social Psychology,* 1970, 16, 12–19.

10 R. W. BUCK, V. J. SAVIN, R. E. MILLER, AND W. F. CAUL, "Communication of Affect Through Facial Expressions in Humans," *Journal of Personality and Social Psychology,* 1972, 23, 362–371.

11 K. DUNLAP, "The Role of Eye-Muscles and Mouth-Muscles in the Expression of the Emotions," *Genetic Psychology Monographs,* 1927, 2, 199–233.

12 P. EKMAN, W. V. FRIESEN, AND P. ELLSWORTH, *op. cit.,* Chapter 17, Part A.

13 P. EKMAN, "Facial Expressions of Emotion," p. 251.

14 P. EKMAN, W. V. FRIESEN, AND P. ELLSWORTH, *op. cit.,* Chapter 17, Part B.

15 M. G. CLINE, "The Influence of Social Context on the Perception of Faces," *Journal of Personality,* 1956, 2, 142–158.

16 N. H. FRIJDA, "Recognition of Emotion," in L. Berkowitz (Ed.), *Advances in Experimental Social Psychology,* Vol. 4 (New York: Academic Press, 1969), pp. 167–223.

17 S. G. WATSON, "Judgment of Emotion From Facial and Contextual Cue Combinations," *Journal of Personality and Social Psychology,* 1972, 24, 334–342.

18 P. EKMAN, W. V. FRIESEN, AND P. ELLSWORTH, *op. cit.,* Chapter 18.

19 *Ibid.,* Chapter 19.

20 P. EKMAN, "Facial Expressions of Emotion."

21 D. E. Bugental, J. W. KASWAN, and L. R. LOVE, "Perception of Contradictory Meanings Conveyed by Verbal and Nonverbal Channels," *Journal of Personality and Social Psychology,* 1970, 16, 647–655.

22 D. E. BUGENTAL, L. R. LOVE, and R. M. GIANETTO, "Perfidious Feminine Faces," *Journal of Personality and Social Psychology,* 1971, 17, 314–318.

23 D. E. BUGENTAL, L. R. LOVE, J. W. KASWAN, and C. APRIL, "Verbal-Nonverbal Conflict in Parental Messages to Normal and Disturbed Children," *Journal of Abnormal Psychology,* 1971, 77, 6–10.

24 P. EKMAN, W. V. FRIESEN, and P. ELLSWORTH, *op. cit.,* p. i.

6

The Voice's Hidden Language

The impressions that we form by listening to people speaking come from three general sources. The first, of course, has to do with what they are saying. We also gain impressions of people from the tone of voice they are using and from their speech patterns, such as how fast they talk and how and when they hesitate or pause. The importance of the voice in first impressions is pointed out clearly in McGinniss's *The Selling of the President 1968*:

> The announcer who was to do the opening called to ask if his tone was too shrill. "Yeah, we don't want it like a quiz show," Roger Ailes said. "He's going to be presidential tonight so announce presidentially." [1]

In 1941 people in various parts of the United States were asked to rate twelve samples of American dialects and one foreign accent. The foreign accent and the New York accent made the most unfavorable impressions. [2] These particular results may not be true today, but we all know that a person's tone of voice or pattern of speaking can have a strong effect on the first impressions that we form.

Research studies done on judgments of voice in the 1930's and 1940's did not make the distinction between voice tone and voice pattern. They were concerned primarily with the question of whether or not we can accurately tell things about other people by listening to them speak. First we will look at some of these studies and consider their strengths and weaknesses. Then we will learn about how voice tones and patterns have been investigated in more recent years.

HOW ACCURATELY CAN WE JUDGE PEOPLE
FROM THEIR VOICES?

The basic procedure of early voice research was to have judges listen to speakers over an intercom system and then make ratings about the speakers on various qualities or traits. Virtually all of these investigations used male speakers. Some of the characteristics that the judges tried to predict from the speakers' voices were age, height, appearance in a photograph, body build, intelligence, leadership ability, and personality traits such as dominance, introversion-extroversion, and sociability.[3] It can generally be concluded from early voice studies that it is easier to make predictions about a person's physical characteristics from his tone of voice than about his personality. This is not surprising because a person's body build has a direct effect on what his or her voice will sound like. It was recently shown, for example, that judges were much more accurate in guessing how forceful and assertive a speaker felt himself to be than they were in predicting how the speaker would rate himself on agility, orderliness, and seriousness.[4]

There are two problems with research studies trying to relate personal characteristics and tone of voice that make the interpretation of their results confusing. First, there is usually no control for how accurate judges might be in their predictions purely from knowledge of stereotypes. For instance, you could be fairly accurate in judging a speaker's height, knowing that he is a male college student, just by guessing that he is about as tall as the average male college student. You could also be reasonably accurate in predicting a speaker's personality traits if you chose traits you knew were typical of most people of the background from which the speaker comes.[5]

A second issue that comes up in studies judging personal characteristics from tone and pattern of voice is that judges may agree among themselves on how to rate a person from his voice, but the ratings may have little to do with what the person is really like. This isn't a completely meaningless finding because it shows that there might be certain types of people whom we are taught (rightly or wrongly) to associate with various kinds of voices. A study of people's reactions to voice qualities found the following stereotypes to exist: Males with breathiness in their voice were seen as younger and more artistic. Females with breathiness gave the impression of being pretty, feminine, petite, high-strung, and shallow. Flatness in the voice was associated with masculinity, sluggishness, and coldness in both males and females. Nasality was perceived as largely undesirable. Males with tenseness in their voice were evaluated as older, unyielding, and cantankerous. Females with tense voices came across as young, emotional, high-strung, and less intelligent. Increased rate of speaking made both males and females appear animated and extroverted. Increased pitch variety gave males a dynamic, feminine, and aesthetically inclined identification. Females with a wide pitch variety appeared dynamic and extroverted.[6]

Other kinds of stereotypes have been associated with people's accents. French and English Canadians were asked to judge people from their voices on a tape recording. Both French and English Canadians preferred the people with English Canadian accents over those using French Canadian accents. Speakers with an English Canadian accent were rated more favorably by English and French Canadians on intelligence, likability, dependability, and character.[7] In another study, Jewish and gentile students tended to devalue a speaker on height, good looks, and leadership when he spoke English with a Jewish accent rather than with a standard American accent. Jewish students, but not gentile students, rated the speaker with the Jewish accent more favorably on sense of humor, entertainingness, and kindness.[8]

Because of the confusion caused by stereotyping, current research on voice tone and voice pattern has focused more on what sorts of impressions we form of people from their voices rather than on how accurately we can make predictions about them. Research on first impressions from voice can be divided into studies of speech patterns and studies of voice tone.

FIRST IMPRESSIONS FROM SPEECH PATTERNS

As suggested earlier, patterns of speech include factors such as how fast or often people speak and how often and when their speech has pauses, hesitations, or disruptions. One method used by psychologists to measure speech patterns in two-person interactions is to have an observer press one button when one person talks and a second button when the other person talks. These buttons are connected to clocks and counters that can give information about a number of different things. The overall amount of talking for each person can be measured, as well as the length and number of separate statements that are made. Information can also be recorded about the number of times each person breaks a silence, how much a person talks relative to how much he or she listens, how often one person interrupts the other, how often an interrupted person yields to the other, and how often one person responds directly or fails to respond to a statement of the other. Since people's patterns of speaking are fairly stable, the various measures described above have good reliability. Several different observers recording the same interaction can agree quite closely about what speech patterns are taking place.[9,10,11]

The above measures of speech patterns have been used in studies of interviews by having an interviewer vary his behavior, such as by being either critical or accepting, or by responding immediately versus remaining silent. Measurements of the speech patterns of the people being interviewed were then compared to see how they were affected by the interviewer's different behaviors.[12] A similar type of investigation looked at correlations between the speech patterns of people in an interview and the kinds of things that were being talked about. People who broke silences quickly and tended not to yield when both they and the interviewer spoke at the same time were more oriented toward interpersonal interaction. People who submitted to interruptions by the interviewer and hesitated to break silences were more likely to be oriented toward themselves and not so interested in interaction with others.[13]

The notion that people tend to talk faster when they are anxious has been supported in two experiments that used number of words spoken per minute as a measure of speech pattern. In one case people were found to talk faster when they were expecting to receive a shock at any moment than when they were not threatened by shock. In another case, people talked more rapidly when they were being interviewed on issues where they had personal problems and less rapidly when the interview was on topics where they felt well adjusted.[14,15]

Another way to study speech patterns objectively is to record the number of speech disturbances that occur while a person is talking. Speech disturbances have been measured by having judges listen to tape recordings of someone speaking and scoring the number of times the person speaking vacillates on words for the same meaning, repeats the same word twice, stutters, omits part of a word, doesn't complete a sentence, and makes slips of the tongue. It has been shown that people have a much greater number of speech disturbances when they are anxious and when they are talking about difficult or embarrassing topics. Analysis of speech disturbances can be made with fairly high agreement between different judges. The method has been used by psychotherapists as a way of assessing the anxiety levels of their patients during therapy sessions.[16,17]

In recent years a growing number of sophisticated studies of voice patterns have been carried out using spectrographic analysis or "voice prints." We won't talk too much about this research here because our interest is on first impressions of people we meet and the discriminations made by these electronic devices are more complex than we can make with our own ears. One study using computer analysis of voice qualities found results that were duplicated by ratings of human judges. Sound tapes were made of a speaker giving a short speech and displaying either confidence or doubt in what he was saying. A computer analysis of the speaker's voice patterns showed that his voice was significantly louder, and that he spoke with significantly shorter pauses and significantly faster rate when he was expressing confidence rather than doubt. Judges who listened to the speaker's voice made similar ratings of his speaking pattern. When the speaker's voice was confident the judges also rated him as significantly more enthusiastic, forceful, active, competent, dominant, self-confident, and self-assured, as compared with those moments when his voice was doubtful.[18]

A relatively straightforward way in which to study speech patterns is to measure the amount of speaking people do in interactions. Several investigations have been conducted in which people were put together in groups and given a topic to discuss or a problem to solve. Sometimes the people had met briefly before and sometimes they had never met. After the discussion the participants were asked to choose a leader or representative for their group. For the most part, the people who had done the most talking during the group discussion were most often chosen as leaders.[19,20,21] The kind of study that puts people together and then finds out that those who talk the most are most often designated as leaders is not fully conclusive, though, because people who talk a lot may have other desirable characteristics which cause them to be chosen. To get around this problem, a more controlled experiment was conducted in which different amounts of talking were identified with the same person. Judges made ratings in a three-person discussion. For some judges Person A talked most of the time, Person B talked a medium amount, and Person C talked least. Other judges heard Person C talk the most and Person A talk the least. Still other judges heard Person B talk the most, and so on. In this way the personal characteristics of the people doing the talking could be separated from the actual amount that they talked. It turned out that people were rated as being the best leaders when they talked the most, but they were liked the best when they talked a medium amount.[22]

A similar experiment had male and female judges listen to a taped conversation between a male and female college student. Judges were told that the students had signed up to be in a study of first impressions. It was explained that the students had just been introduced and placed in a room with a tape recorder to "get to know each other" and talk about anything they wished. The judges' task was to pay attention to either the male or the female and then give their impressions of the person on a rating form. The conversations had been electronically filtered in such a way that the speakers' voice tones could be easily distinguished but the words they spoke could not. This was done to insure that the judges would base their evaluations on the tone of the person they listened to rather than on what he or she said.

Unbeknownst to the judges, the same male and female made three different recordings. In one recording, the male talked 80 percent of the time and the female talked 20 percent of the time. In a second recording, the female talked 80 percent of the time and the male talked 20 percent of the time. In a third recording, the male and female each talked 50 percent of the time. Each judge listened to one recording.

Results of the study showed a significant tendency for both male and female judges to rate males and females who talked 80 percent of the time as most warm, friendly, intelligent, and outgoing. The males and females who spoke 20 percent of the time were rated as most cold, unfriendly, unintelligent, and introverted. In addition, males who talked 80 percent of the time were rated by judges as being significantly more inconsiderate, impolite, and inattentive than all other male and female speakers.

The fact that only males suffered these negative ratings for talking too much is interesting. One possible explanation is that males are assumed to have more power in a conversation with a female and if they talk too much it seems they are not giving the poor woman a chance. If the female talks a lot, it is presumably all right because the male is "allowing" her to do so. Another explanation is that females are typically seen as being more sensitive and understanding than males. If females talk a lot it maybe thought that it is in order to make a male who is shy more comfortable.[23]

A study in which female students interviewed male students indicated that the males preferred the female interviewers who talked the most. This was probably because the males felt a little less "on the spot" when the interviewer helped to break periods of silence by increasing her amount of talking.[24]

Females who are identified on personality scales as extroverts have been found to spend significantly more time in speaking and significantly less time in silence than females who are identified as introverts.[25] Psychotic and neurotic patients speak much less in an interview than do normal people.[26]

Speech patterns of interviewers can influence the speech patterns of people being interviewed. If the interviewer increases the length of his statements, the person being interviewed will also lengthen his statements. If the interviewer nods his head or says "Mm-hmm" he can get the person being interviewed to talk for longer periods of time.[27]

FIRST IMPRESSIONS FROM TONE OF VOICE

In order to study reactions to a person's tone of voice we have to separate *what* the person is saying from *how* he or she is saying it. Most of the time the words a person uses express the same feelings as his or her tone of voice. Sometimes, however, people try to hide their true feelings behind words and there is a discrepancy between what they say and how they say it. In these cases we are often more accurate in understanding their true feelings if we can concentrate on their tone of voice without being distracted or misled by the specific words being spoken. Several studies have shown cases in which people were more accurate in making judgments about someone else when they heard his or her tone of voice, rather than only reading a transcript of the words the person had spoken. In one case, judges who heard actual voices were more efficient in differentiating personality types of people who were speaking in an aggressive situation than judges who only read the words that were spoken.[28] In another case, judges were more accurate in predicting how other people would complete a series of sentences if they previously had heard their voices in an interview rather than just reading a transcript of the interview.[29]

There are two general methods used by studies of tone of voice to separate the words a person is speaking from the tone of voice he or she is using. One method is to have people attempt to portray different emotions in their voices while speaking words or sentences whose content is standard or neutral. A second approach is electronically to filter tape recordings of people speaking so that their words can no longer be understood but the tones in their voices can still be discriminated.

Removing Word Content with Standardized Speech. Four men and four women recited the alphabet ten times, each time trying to communicate a different emotion in their voices. The emotions of anger, fear, happiness, jealousy, love, nervousness, pride, sadness, satisfaction, and sympathy were portrayed in different orders by the speakers to balance out effects of practice. When judges listened to tape recordings of the speakers they were able to guess all ten emotions with an accuracy beyond chance. Anger was the easiest emotion to identify and pride was the most difficult. There was a fairly large variation between the judges in how accurate they were and between the speakers in how clearly they conveyed the emotions.[30] Two speakers in a second study expressed fifty different feelings by reciting the alphabet. Tones of voice for feelings similar to each other (such as anger and jealousy or fear and nervousness) were much more difficult for judges to tell apart than voice tones for feelings not similar. Negative and positive feelings in voice tone were equally easy to judge.[31]

A comparison of emotional communication through speech, art, and music led to some interesting findings. Speakers read the following paragraph into a tape recorder: "I am going out now. I won't be back all afternoon. If anyone calls, just tell them I'm not here." Each time the speakers read the paragraph they used tones of voice that would convey ten different emotions: admiration, amusement, anger, boredom, despair, disgust, fear, impatience, joy, and love. In addition, artists were asked to create abstract representations of the emotions read by the speakers and musicians were given the task of communicating the emotions in short improvisations on the instrument of their choice. Judges who made ratings about which emotions were being expressed by the speakers, artists, and musicians had an agreement well beyond chance. Because the ten emotions could be communicated in a parallel fashion in speech, art, and music, it was concluded that emotional expression is a relatively stable and general human characteristic. Judges who rated themselves as being sensitive toward other people were more accurate in their ratings of speakers and artists (but not musicians) than judges who felt they were not particularly sensitive toward others. There was no difference between men and women in ability to make judgments of the emotions.[32]

Two other studies have led to the conclusion that emotional communication is a general human ability. In one case, it was shown that people who have high accuracy in conveying emotions through their own speech are very skillful in judging emotions in the speech of others.[33] People who are skillful in expressing emotions in their voice can also express emotions very accurately with their face. There is no apparent difference between men and women in ability to convey and perceive emotions in tone of voice and facial expression.[34]

One way to determine the influence of learning and experience on vocal communication of emotion is to study children at various ages. It has been shown that children at age five can interpret emotions in voice with better than chance accuracy. As children increase in age to twelve years, their accuracy in judging tone of voice becomes consistently higher.[35] A second way to measure the effects of experience on vocal communication is to compare groups of people from different backgrounds. Blind and sighted adolescents were compared in their abilities to identify emotions in tone of voice from the standardized paragraph quoted earlier. Results showed that sighted adolescents were more accurate in identifying vocal emotions than were blind adolescents. This might be somewhat unexpected if we consider that blind people possibly have developed more sensitive hearing in order to compensate for their visual handicap. However, it is also true that blind people have less chance to get feedback from others about expressions of emotions. Their contact with a wide range of voice tones and expressions is limited.[36] Patients who are diagnosed as schizophrenic are less accurate than normal people in identifying emotions in tone of voice. This might also be due to the fact that schizophrenics have limited or even maladaptive experience in learning emotional expressions in tone of voice.[37]

A slightly different method using standardized speech is to have actors read passages that have been written to emphasize certain emotions. A passage may consist of a very angry story, to emphasize anger, or of a very sad story, to emphasize sadness, and so on. One sentence in each of the passages is the same so that it can be isolated on a recording and played to judges. A study using this method found that people could identify the emotions of contempt, anger, fear, grief, and indifference with very high accuracy. Analysis of the pitch characteristics of the different emotions showed some interesting findings. Emotions of anger and fear were expressed in a much higher pitched voice than emotions of contempt and grief. Indifference was expressed in the lowest pitched voice. Voices expressing contempt, anger, and fear had a wider range of changes in pitch and inflection than voices of grief and indifference. There were also differences in the various emotions in terms of rate of speaking. Fear, anger, and indifference were expressed with a much faster speaking rate than contempt and grief. Voices of contempt were characterized by a very slow but steady rate of speech. Voices of grief had an especially large number of pauses, both within phrases and between phrases.[38,39]

Removing Word Content with Electronic Filtering. Tape-recorded conversations can be played through an electronic filter which allows only frequencies in the vicinity of 100 to 500 cycles per second to be heard. If this is done, the tones of voice in the conversations can still be discriminated but the exact words being spoken are muddled and no longer understood.[40] The advantage of electronic filtering in studying voice tone is that any tape-recorded conversation can be used. Research is not limited to specifically prepared tapes as it is with the method of standardized speech. One investigation using this technique had judges listen to electronically filtered tapes of Senator Joseph McCarthy and the lawyer Joseph Welch that were made during the 1954 Army-McCarthy hearings. Judgments of the two men's voice tones were matched with what they were saying. Results showed that Mr. Welch's voice quality varied much more with the content of his speech than did Senator McCarthy's. McCarthy's voice had little variation in tone, even when he was speaking about emotional issues.[41] We can see how electronic filtering might be used for studying individual differences between people. A second way to remove word content from taped conversations is to cut the tape up into segments and then splice the segments back together in a random order. This method has an advantage over electronic filtering because none of the frequencies of the original conversation are distorted. It is also possible to play randomly spliced tapes to people many different times without them being able to figure out what is being said. If it is desirable to make judges unaware of speech patterns, such as pauses, these can be taken out of the tape before it is spliced back together.[42]

THE VOICE AND HUMAN INTERACTION

Since many of our interactions with other people involve speaking, it is not surprising that patterns and tones of voice would have some effect on their outcome. One series of research studies attempted to find out whether the ability to comprehend or remember what someone says has anything to do with his or her manner of speaking. Messages were transmitted to audiences in voices that were varied along a number of different dimensions. Voices were monotonous or varied in pitch and were smooth or broken with pauses or stuttering. Messages were spoken at a normal or at a very fast rate. The general conclusion of these studies was that extreme tones and patterns in voices are somewhat unpleasant to listeners, but they do not markedly reduce understanding of what is being said.

Although listeners may not like the particular way in which a person is speaking, they can usually make out the message if they are interested.[43]

An area of interaction in which the voice does play an important part is that of persuasion. People can be more effective in changing attitudes of others if they speak in a voice that makes them appear credible. Tapes were made of speeches that contained varying amounts of interruptions, such as "ahs," sentence corrections, stuttering, repetitions, and tongue slips. Speakers were rated more and more incompetent as the number of interruptions in their speech increased.[44,45] In another investigation, a speaker presented an argument in which his voice was either objective and calm or emotional and involved. The calm voice had a smaller range of inflections, more consistency in rate and pitch, and was lower in volume and tone than the excited voice. The speeches were electronically filtered and played to judges who gave their impressions of the person giving the speech. The speaker was rated as significantly more trustworthy and likable when he spoke in an objective rather than emotional manner. The objective speaker was also seen as more attractive, better educated, taller, of a higher income level, more honest, and more people-oriented than the emotional speaker. The emotional speaker came across to judges as more tough-minded, task-oriented, self-assured, and assertive.[46]

Speakers who are consciously trying to be persuasive have been shown to talk faster and with more intonation and volume than speakers who are trying to be neutral.[47] Speakers who were being deceitful and giving an argument with which they did not agree were compared with truthful speakers who were presenting an argument which they did believe. Deceitful speakers said less, made more speech errors, and spoke more slowly than truthful speakers.[48]

Tones and patterns of voice can be influential in an interaction as subtle as the giving of instructions for an experiment. Tape recordings were made of experimenters as they gave instructions to participants in a study who were about to make ratings of photographs. Careful scoring of the experimenters' voices showed that the way in which they emphasized certain parts of the instructions with different stress and voice pitch had a significant effect on how the participants in the study carried out their ratings.[49,50]

The voice also has an important relationship to the success of psychotherapy. Tape recordings were collected of psychotherapy sessions that were felt by therapists to have been very successful or rather poor. The voices of the psychotherapists in the sessions were then carefully scored by judges to see what differences there might have been between the successful and the poor sessions. During successful psychotherapy sessions the voices of psychotherapists tended to have a medium or normal amount of intensity and stress and a soft, relaxed, warm tone. In the poorer psychotherapy sessions the therapists' voices more often had a flat sound or a monotone. If the voices of the therapists became more intense they communicated more a sense of editorializing or speaking for effect than one of warmth or relaxation. The psychotherapists also had more pauses in their speech and uttered more "uhs" and "uhms" during the poor sessions than during the successful ones. This study doesn't tell us anything about how the patients reacted to the different speaking patterns of the psychotherapists, but it does show that the psychotherapists' view of whether a psychotherapy session is successful has something to do with the nature of their voice patterns during the session.[51]

When confronted for the first time with a tape recording of their voice, most persons react with immediate discomfort. People pay much more attention to qualities of nasality, rasp, tone, and rhythm when listening to their own voice than listening to voices of others. At first, the feelings about one's own voice are generally negative. This is probably because we are not used to what we hear and also, possibly, because we hear aspects of our feelings and emotions that we had not intended to show. When we become used to hearing our own voice these things don't bother us so much anymore.[52] It is interesting that only 30 percent of average people can correctly identify their voices in a recording. Radio announcers and speakers who have a lot of experience in hearing their own voice are accurate in identifying their voice almost all of the time.[53]

VOCAL EXPRESSIONS IN DIFFERENT CULTURES

In Chapters 4 and 5 we looked at research that has pointed out similarities and differences between cultures in the ways they use and interpret body language, gestures, and facial expressions. Different cultures have also been compared in their interpretations of tone of voice. Tape recordings were made in which Americans spoke words or read sentences with neutral content while they expressed different moods in their tone of voice. The moods which were expressed in the tape recordings were anger, sadness, happiness, flirtatiousness, fear, and indifference. The tapes were played to American college students and to college students in

Japan and Poland. As might be expected, Americans were more accurate in their recognition of the emotions than were students in Poland and Japan, but Polish and Japanese students were also able to identify the emotions on the tapes with an accuracy above chance. It was concluded that there is a good deal of cross-cultural similarity in recognition of emotion from tone of voice. The most difficult emotions for the Japanese and Polish students to identify were flirtatiousness and happiness. The foreign students may have had trouble with identifying a flirting voice because the tone used in such a voice is more specific to each culture or because the definition of the word "flirt" itself is hard to translate into other languages. Generally speaking, the foreign students were more accurate in identifying emotions when the tapes they were given to listen to were at least a sentence long rather than just a couple of words. Americans were able to judge accurately the taped emotions even when they consisted of only one or two words.[54] In another study, students from America, Israel, and Japan recited the alphabet in their own language while expressing emotions of anger, jealousy, love, nervousness, pride, and sadness. Judges who listened to the speakers and rated which emotions were being expressed had equal accuracy for speakers outside of their culture and speakers from their own culture. Again, expressions of emotion in tone of voice seemed to be very similar for different cultures. The easiest emotions to recognize were anger and sadness. The most difficult emotions to communicate by voice tone were nervousness and jealousy.[55]

DO WE LEARN MORE FROM THE FACE OR VOICE?

It stands to reason that if we have both facial and vocal information about a person we can be more accurate in our perceptions than if we are limited to just one or the other. The only time there might be an exception is if the person is being deceitful and sending facial and vocal messages that are in conflict. Judges in a study were asked to rate emotions portrayed on videotapes with sound. The judges either saw the videotape with sound, saw the videotapes without sound, or heard only the sound. Judges were most accurate in rating emotions when they saw the videotapes with sound. Viewing the tapes unaccompanied by sound resulted in more accuracy than hearing the sound only.[56] Participants in another investigation attempted to judge emotions from photographs of faces, from tape-recorded voices, and from photographs and voices combined. The participants were most accurate when they had both the faces and voices to work with. They were about one and a half times more accurate with the faces alone than they were with the voices alone.[57,58]

BECOMING AWARE OF THE VOICE

As you have seen, a good deal of the research in vocal communication has focused on variables that we don't usually discriminate when we interact with other people. Even after reading this chapter, it will be difficult for you to judge how much your first impressions of others are affected by how fast they talk or by their speech disturbances, voice intensities, or voice tones. What might be easier to do is to become aware of how much people talk in a conversation and to whom they direct their statements. We all know how two people demonstrate interest at first meeting by focusing their remarks specifically toward each other. The influence of how much people talk on first impressions is less clear-cut. We have learned about the richness of information that is gained from others through their physical appearance, gaze and distance behaviors, body language, facial expressions, and tone of voice. Yet it is my experience that we don't pursue our first impressions of others unless they are willing to talk to us. Since not much research has been done on amount of talking and first impressions, you might wish to investigate it yourself. When you meet someone for the first time, are you uncomfortable if he or she doesn't talk a lot? Do you develop an anxious feeling during periods of silence, a sense that you ought to be saying something?

NOTES

1 J. McGinniss, *The Selling of the President 1968* (New York: Trident, 1969), p. 155. This statement is also quoted by M. L. Knapp, *Nonverbal Communication in Human Interaction* (New York: Holt, 1972), p. 158.

2 W. Wilke and J. Snyder, "Attitudes Toward American Dialects," *Journal of Social Psychology*, 1941, 14, 349–362.

3 E. Kramer, "Judgment of Personal Characteristics and Emotions from Nonverbal Properties," *Psychological Bulletin*, 1963, 60, 408–420.

4 R. G. Hunt and T. K. Lin, "Accuracy of Judgments of Personal Attributes From Speech," *Journal of Personality and Social Psychology*, 1967, 6, 450–453.

5 W. Mischel, *Personality and Assessment* (New York: Wiley, 1968). A different point of view is presented by E. Kramer, "Personality Stereotypes in Voice: A Reconsideration of the Data," *Journal of Social Psychology*, 1964, 62, 247–251.

6 D. W. ADDINGTON, "The Relationship of Selected Vocal Characteristics to Personality Perception," *Speech Monographs*, 1968, 35, 492–503.

7 W. E. LAMBERT, H. FRANKEL, and G. R. TICKER, "Judging Personality Through Speech: A French-Canadian Example," *Journal of Communication*, 1966, 16, 305–321.

8 M. ANISFELD, N. BOGO, and W. LAMBERT, "Evaluation Reactions to Accented English Speech," *Journal of Abnormal and Social Psychology*, 1962, 65, 223–231.

9 J. S. PHILLIPS, J. D. MATARAZZO, R. G. MATARAZZO, and G. SASLOW, "Observer Reliability of Interaction Patterns During Interviews," *Journal of Consulting Psychology*, 1957, 21, 269–275.

10 G. SASLOW, J. D. MATARAZZO, and S. B. GUZE, "The Stability of Interaction Chronograph Patterns in Psychiatric Interviews," *Journal of Consulting Psychology*, 1955, 19, 417–420.

11 V. B. TUASON, S. B. GUZE, J. McCLURE, and J. BEGUELIN, "A Further Study of Some Features of the Interview With the Interaction Chronograph," *American Journal of Psychiatry*, 1961, 118, 438–446.

12 J. D. MATARAZZO, G. SASLOW, and R. G. MATARAZZO, "The Interaction Chronograph as an Instrument for Objective Measurement of Interaction Patterns During Interviews," *Journal of Psychology*, 1956, 41, 347–367.

13 J. S. PHILLIPS. R. G. MATARAZZO, J. D. MATARAZZO, G. SASLOW, and F. H. KANFER, "Relationships Between Descriptive Content and Interaction Behavior in Interviews," *Journal of Consulting Psychology*, 1961, 25, 260–266.

14 F. H. KANFER, "Effect of a Warning Signal Preceding a Noxious Stimulus on Verbal Rate and Heart Rate," *Journal of Experimental Psychology*, 1958, 55, 73–80.

15 F. H. KANFER, "Verbal Rate, Content, and Adjustment Ratings in Experimentally Structured Interviews," *Journal of Abnormal and Social Psychology*, 1959, 58, 305–311.

16 S. V. KASL and G. F. MAHL, "The Relationship of Disturbances and Hesitations in Spontaneous Speech to Anxiety," *Journal of Personality and Social Psychology*, 1965, 1, 425–433.

17 G. F. MAHL, "Disturbances and Silences in the Patient's Speech in Psychotherapy," *Journal of Abnormal and Social Psychology*, 1956, 53, 1–15.

18 K. R. SCHERER, H. LONDON, and J. J. WOLF, "The Voice of Confidence: Paralinguistic Cues and Audience Evaulation," *Journal of Research in Personality*, 1973, 7, 31–44.

19 B. M. BASS, "An Analysis of the Leaderless Group Discussion," *Journal of Applied Psychology*, 1949, 33, 527–533.

20 E. F. BORGATTA and R. F. BALES, "Sociometric Status Patterns and Characteristics of Interaction," *Journal of Social Psychology*, 1956, 43, 289–297.

21 J. B. KIRSCHT, T. M. LODAHL, AND M. HAIRE, "Some Factors in the Selection of Leaders by Members of Small Groups," *Journal of Abnormal and Social Psychology*, 1959, 58, 406–408.

22 D. J. STANG, "Effect of Interaction Rate on Ratings of Leadership and Liking," *Journal of Personality and Social Psychology*, 1973, 27, 405–408.

23 C. L. KLEINKE, M. R. LENGA, and T. A. BEACH, "Effect of Talking Rate on First Impressions: Do Sex and Attractiveness Make a Difference?" Paper presented at the meeting of the Western Psychological Association, San Francisco, Calif., 1974.

24 C. L. KLEINKE, R. A. STANESKI, and D. E. BERGER, "Evaluation of an Interviewer as a Function of Interviewer Gaze, Reinforcement of Subject Gaze, and Interviewer Attractiveness," *Journal of Personality and Social Psychology*, 1975, 31, 115–122.

25 R. W. RAMSAY, "Personality and Speech," *Journal of Personality and Social Psychology*, 1966, 4, 116–118.

26 J. D. MATARAZZO, A. N. WIENS, and G. SASLOW, "Studies of Interview Speech Behavior," in L. Krasner and L. P. Ullmann (Eds.), *Research in Behavior Modification* (New York: Holt, Rinehart & Winston, 1965), pp. 179–210.

27 *Ibid.*

28 J. STARKWEATHER, "Content-Free Speech as a Souce of Information About the Speaker," *Journal of Abnormal and Social Psychology*, 1956, 52, 394–402.

29 J. LUFT, "Differences in Prediction Based on Hearing Versus Reading Verbatim Clinical Interviews," *Journal of Consulting Psychology*, 1951, 15, 115–119.

30 J. DAVITZ and L. DAVITZ, "The Communication of Feelings by Content-Free Speech," *Journal of Communication*, 1959, 9, 6–13.

31 J. DAVITZ and L. DAVITZ, "Correlates of Accuracy in the Communication of Feelings," *Journal of Communication*, 1959, 9, 110–117.

32 M. BELDOCK, "Sensitivity to Expression of Emotional Meaning in Three Modes of Communication," in J. Davitz (Ed.), *The Communication of Emotional Meaning* (New York: McGraw-Hill, 1964), Chapter 3.

33 P. K. LEVY, "The Ability to Express and Perceive Vocal Communications of Feeling," in Davitz, *op. cit.*, Chapter 4.

34 E. A. LEVITT, "The Relationship Between Abilities to Express Emotional Meanings Vocally and Facially," in J. Davitz, *op. cit.*, Chapter 7.

35 L. DIMITROVSKY, "The Ability to Identify the Emotional Meaning of Vocal Expressions at Successive Age Levels," in J. Davitz, *op. cit.*, Chapter 6.

36 S. BLAU, "An Ear for an Eye: Sensory Compensation and Judgments of Affect by the Blind," in J. Davitz, *op. cit.*, Chapter 9.

37 J. B. TURNER, "Schizophrenics as Judges of Vocal Expressions of Emotional Meaning," in J. Davitz, *op. cit.*, Chapter 10.

38 G. FAIRBANKS and W. PROVENOST, "An Experimental Study of the Pitch Characteristics of the Voice During the Expression of Emotion," *Speech Monographs*, 1939, 6, 87–104.

39 G. FAIRBANKS and L. W. HOAGLIN, "An Experimental Study of the Durational Characteristics of the Voice During Expression of Emotion," *Speech Monographs*, 1941, 8, 85–90.

40 J. STARKWEATHER, "Content-Free Speech as a Source of Information About the Speaker."

41 J. STARKWEATHER, "The Communication Value of Content-Free Speech," *American Journal of Psychology*, 1956, 69, 121–123.

42 K. R. SCHERER, "Randomized Splicing: A Note on a Simple Technique for Masking Speech Content," *Journal of Experimental Research in Personality*, 1971, 5, 155–159.

43 M. L. KNAPP, *Nonverbal Communication in Human Interaction* (New York: Holt, Rinehart & Winston, 1972), pp. 165–166.

44 K. K. SERENO and G. J. HAWKINS, "The Effect of Variations in Speakers' Noninfluency Upon Audience Ratings of Attitude Toward the Speech Topic and Speakers' Credibility," *Speech Monographs*, 1967, 34, 58–64.

45 G. R. MILLER and M. A. HEWGILL, "The Effect of Variations in Noninfluency on Audience Ratings of Source Credibility," *Quarterly Journal of Speech*, 1964, 50, 36–44.

46 W. B. PEARCE and F. CONKLIN, "Nonverbal Vocalic Communication and Perceptions of a Speaker," *Speech Monographs*, 1971, 38, 235–241.

47 A. MEHRABIAN and M. WILLIAMS, "Nonverbal Concomitants of Perceived and Intended Persuasiveness," *Journal of Personality and Social Psychology*, 1969, 13, 37–58.

48 A. MEHRABIAN, "Nonverbal Betrayal of Feeling," *Journal of Experimental Research in Personality*, 1971, 5, 64–73.

49 S. D. DUNCAN, M. J. ROSENBERG, and J. FINKELSTEIN, "The Paralanguage of Experimenter Bias," *Sociometry*, 1969, 32, 207–219.

50 S. D. DUNCAN and R. ROSENTHAL, "Vocal Emphasis in Experimenters' Introduction Reading as Unintended Determinant of Subjects' Responses," *Language and Speech*, 1968, 11, 20–26.

51 S. D. DUNCAN, L. N. RICE, and J. M. BUTLER, "Therapists' Paralanguage in Peak and Poor Psychotherapy Hours," *Journal of Abnormal Psychology*, 1968, 73, 566–570.

52 P. S. HOLZMAN and C. ROUSEY, "The Voice as a Percept," *Journal of Personality and Social Psychology*, 1966, 4, 79–86.

53 C. ROUSEY and P. S. HOLZMAN, "Recognition of One's Own Voice," *Journal of Personality and Social Psychology*, 1967, 6, 464–466.

54 E. G. BEIER and A. ZAUTRA, "Identification of Vocal Communication of Emotions Across Cultures," Mimeographed paper, University of Utah, 1972.

55 J. DAVITZ, "Minor Studies and Some Hypotheses," in J. Davitz, *op. cit.*, Chapter 11.

56 K. L. BURNS and E. G. BEIER, "Decoding of Emotional Meaning: I. Characteristics of Vocal Versus Visual Cues II. Comparisons of Normal and Deaf Children," Mimeographed paper, University of Utah, 1972.

57 A. MEHRABIAN and S. R. FERRIS, "Inferences of Attitudes from Nonverbal Communication in Two Channels," *Journal of Consulting Psychology*, 1967, 31, 248–252.

58 S. F. ZAIDEL and A. MEHRABIAN, "The Ability to Communicate and Infer Positive and Negative Attitudes Facially and Vocally," *Journal of Experimental Research in Personality*, 1969, 3, 233–241.

7

Do Opposites Attract?

If you think about it for a while you will find that people who are close to you share many more similarities than differences. It is true that we are sometimes also attracted to very different or unusual people, but this is more often the exception than the rule. Our tendency to prefer people who are similar to us can be seen as a product of many factors. Having friends who are similar to us provides balance and consistency in our lives, which is felt by many psychologists to be an important human motive. People who are similar are reinforcing because they support our beliefs and serve as a favorable standard against which we can judge ourselves. People who are similar are also more likely to be attracted to us and this creates a positive feeling that makes us like them in return.[1]

LIKES LIKE LIKES

Research studies provide a wide range of examples showing a positive relationship between similarity and interpersonal attraction.[2] In the 1930's husbands and wives were compared with randomly paired men and women of similar age, education, and cultural background. Married couples had considerably more similarity than random couples in age, height, weight, arithmetic reasoning, and knowledge of current events.[3] Other studies showed that husbands and wives had high similarity in their attitudes toward issues involving religion, economics, education, and politics. Married couples also expressed significant agreement on values such as cheerfulness, cleanliness, friendliness, obedience, and respect.[4] A more recent study conducted in the 1970's found that husbands and wives were in significantly closer agreement on sexual issues than were randomly paired men and women.[5] Couples who are happily married have higher agreement than unhappy and divorced couples on how to deal with arguments, what sort of work they prefer doing, and the hobbies and free-time activities they like to pursue.[6,7] White people in the U.S. marry other whites 99.8 percent of the time. Blacks marry fellow blacks 99 percent of the time. Husbands and wives in the U.S. belong to the same religious group in 93.6 percent of all marriages, whereas only 56 percent of American couples would be expected to share the same religion by chance.[8] A study of college dating couples showed that couples were much more likely to become engaged or married if they agreed closely on attitudes toward marriage, family, and children than if they did not.[9]

As we noted earlier, people who are friends also have more similarity to each other than people who are not friends. Friends share considerably more agreement on economic, aesthetic, social, political, racial, and religious issues than do unacquainted people.[10,11] A survey asking 1,000 men to describe their best friends found an overwhelming tendency for friends to be similar in economic, religious, and social background.[12]

During the election for mayor in New York City, male pedestrians were asked for their voting choice: Lindsay (six foot three) or Procaccino (five foot six). In a significant majority of cases, men who preferred Lindsay were taller than men who favored Procaccino. Male friends have been shown to be closer in height than males from the same background who are randomly matched.[13]

The research that we have considered so far does not permit us to conclude that similarity between people causes them to like each other. It may be that people like each other first and then become more similar as a result of their liking—except, of course, in the matter of size! In order to test whether or not similarity increases liking it is necessary to introduce people to each other, systematically vary the amount of similarity or dissimilarity between them, and then measure how much they like each other. A large number of research studies have attempted to do this. We can look now at what they found.

REACTIONS TOWARD A DEVIANT

College students were brought together in discussion groups in which they were given a case involving a juvenile delinquent and asked to decide what should be done with him. Should he be punished or should he be given consideration and love? Unbeknownst to the students, one of the participants in each group was a confederate of the experimenter and intentionally took a position that would disagree with the views of the rest of the group. Students generally favored moderate to light punishment for the delinquent, but the confederate always argued for very severe punishment. At first the students directed most of their attention toward the "deviant" by speaking to him and listening to what he had to say. When it became apparent during the conversation that the confederate was not going to change his views, the group began to ignore him. By the end of the discussion the students spoke very little to the deviant and gave him little chance to speak to them. When the students were asked to rate how much they liked each other and whom they would like to be with in future discussion groups they consistently rejected the deviant. In other group discussions a confederate would first take a deviant position and then change his statements to agree with the group during the course of the discussion. When the confederate took this "slider" role the other students did not reject and dislike him at the end of the discussion. Apparently it is all right to be dissimilar at the onset of a conversation if you are willing to change your views to agree with the group as the discussion goes on. To remain dissimilar in your views puts you in jeopardy of being disliked and rejected from future discussions.[14]

THE PHANTOM OTHER

One widely used technique for measuring the effects of similarity on liking is to place people in a situation in which they are expecting to meet someone previously unknown to them. Before being introduced the participants are given information describing their prospective partner as being either similar or dissimilar on a number of possible dimensions. The participants are then asked to predict how much they think they will like the person whom they will be meeting by filling out a rating form. Because the participants make ratings of a similar or dissimilar person they have never met, the hypothetical person is called the "phantom other." With this technique the effects of similarity on liking can be studied without interference from factors such as physical appearance, tone of voice, body language, and facial expression. The general finding of phantom other studies is that liking for people increases as they appear more similar and decreases as they appear more dissimilar.[15]

Many studies using the phantom other technique have varied how similar or dissimilar a hypothetical person is in attitudes on issues such as belief in God, birth control, careers for women, drinking, and entertainment. Whether the issues in question were important to the participants or not, the more similar the other person was, the more he or she was liked. People who appeared to become increasingly similar in their attitudes when information was given over time were liked more and more. People who appeared to become increasingly dissimilar in their attitudes over time were liked less and less.[16]

People have also been found to like others more when they are similar in their judgments and similar in the ways they behave. People like others better who are similar on various personality dimensions. Even disagreeable people are liked better if they are similar rather than dissimilar. Similarity influences liking of others whether they are of either high or low prestige. Similarity is important for liking whether the other person is physically attractive or unattractive. Similarity determines how much we like people of the same or opposite sex and people of our race and other races.[17]

When participants in studies are exposed to people expressing similar or dissimilar attitudes in video or audio recordings they prefer the people who are similar. When people are introduced face-to-face they are more favorable toward each other when they have attitudes which are similar.[18]

SIMILARITY IN DIFFERENT POPULATIONS

Psychological research is sometimes questioned when it focuses exclusively on the study of college students. The tendency for people to prefer others who are similar has been shown to hold as well for primary and secondary school children, clerical workers, surgical patients, alcoholics, schizophrenics, and Job Corps trainees. Studies in the U.S., Japan, India, and Mexico have found the same result.[19]

SOME POSSIBLE EXCEPTIONS

We have seen that there is a tendency in diverse populations for people to prefer others who are similar in attitudes, judgments, personality, and behavior. Are there any exceptions? Certainly we might prefer someone who is dissimilar if he or she is extremely attractive or possesses other especially favorable characteristics. What if a person similar to us is emotionally disturbed? Wouldn't we like a dissimilar normal person better? Favoring a disturbed person who is similar to us might imply that we too are disturbed. Studies that have been conducted to test this question have found that people do prefer a similar person who is normal over a similar person who is emotionally disturbed. However, people also like a disturbed person who is similar better than they like a normal person who is dissimilar. Possibly, people identify with a similar person who is emotionally disturbed and feel sorry for him or her. In any case, the influence of similarity on liking holds even when we look at people with somewhat negative qualities.[20]

One study showing an exception to people's preference for similar others found that a similar person who is highly obnoxious is not liked as well as a dissimilar person who is pleasant.[21] We can conclude that a dissimilar person may be preferred over a similar person when the dissimilar person has other very positive attributes or when the similar person has other very negative attributes. In most cases, however, similar people will be liked better than dissimilar people.

PREFERENCE FOR SIMILARITY HAS IMPORTANT CONSEQUENCES

The fact that we tend to like people who are similar to us more than we like people who are dissimilar has important consequences for how we get along and interact with others is our everyday lives. In addition to liking similar people better, we also give them favor in numerous other ways. One study showed, for example, that participants were much more likely to go out of their way to help another person who held similar rather than dissimilar attitudes.[22] Not surprisingly, perhaps, people view similar others as being more intelligent, more knowledgeable, better adjusted, and of higher morality than dissimilar others.[23] When people are asked for their voting preference, they choose candidates who are described as similar rather than dissimilar.[24] Participants in a study were placed in bargaining situations in which they had to come to terms with an opponent who was either similar or dissimilar on a number of attitudes. There was significantly more cooperation in the interactions when the participants' attitudes were similar rather than dissimilar.[25] People in an emergency situation were shown to model their reactions much more after a similar person who was with them than a dissimilar person who was with them.[26]

Participants in a study carried on a conversation with another person who expressed attitudes either similar or dissimilar to their own. When the other person was dissimilar the participants became significantly more aroused physiologically.[27] In another study, people worked on a task with another person who had similar or dissimilar attitudes. When the other person was similar, people estimated that time was passing much more quickly and that the interaction was much more enjoyable than when the other person was dissimilar.[28] When people were asked to evaluate the performance of another person on a learning task they gave higher ratings to a person who was similar than to one who was dissimilar even though the performances were exactly the same.[29] People have also been shown to learn better when they perceive a teacher who reinforces them as similar to themselves.[30]

College students were matched with a date who was either similar or dissimilar in attitudes on a number of topics. Students consistently liked similar dates better than dissimilar dates. Students also felt that similar dates were more intelligent, more desirable as dates, and more desirable as marriage partners.[31]

A study of school principals found that they had a strong preference for hiring teachers who held beliefs similar to their own. Similarity in beliefs was much more important to the principals in making their choices than the amount of experience the teachers had.[32] People making decisions on hiring undergraduate research assistants were also shown to base their hiring and salary recommendations on how similar the applicants' attitudes were to their own.[33]

When business students were asked to decide who should get loans they overwhelmingly chose applicants who had similar attitudes.[34] People who were asked to decide on a sentence for a convicted murderer gave significantly lighter sentences to a murderer who had attitudes similar to theirs.[35] People acting as judges in another study were given a fixed amount of evidence about a defendant and asked to decide whether or not he was guilty. The judges were more likely to find the defendant guilty when he had dissimilar attitudes, even though the evidence was exactly the same. Dissimilar defendants were also given longer sentences and lower ratings on intelligence, morality, adjustment, and goodness, compared with defendants who had attitudes similar to those of the judges.[36]

The pervading influence of similarity on liking for others might remind you of the powerful effects of physical attractiveness that were discussed in Chapter 1. It is likely that similarity is of more lasting influence in the formation of impressions than attractiveness. We might get used to liking people who are not so good-looking after we get to know them better. It is not as likely that we will come to like someone who consistently remains dissimilar to us. But we can also look at this issue in another way. Even though the positive effects of similarity are more long-lasting than those of attractiveness, there is more that we can do to achieve them. The most we can do in terms of physical attractiveness is to get a face lift or buy some new clothes. That is not a terribly humanizing prospect. Learning to increase our appreciation for dissimilar people, on the other hand, provides us with an exciting and potentially self-fulfilling challenge.

LEARNING TO APPRECIATE DISSIMILARITY

Increasing Empathy. To empathize with other people means to place yourself in their life and view the world from their perspective.

David Rosenhan and his colleagues attempted to experience the life of mental patients by getting themselves admitted as patients to a total of twelve mental hospitals throughout the U. S. Rosenhan and his colleagues called the hospitals for an appointment and when they came for an interview they complained that they had been hearing voices. This alleged symptom was enough to get all of the "pseudopatients" admitted as patients, usually with a diagnosis of schizophrenia. The average stay for each of the pseudopatients was nineteen days. After being admitted to the various hospitals the pseudopatients made no attempt to behave in an abnormal manner. Because they had a label of schizophrenia, however, they were never detected as "normal" by the hospital psychiatrists and staff members. Interestingly, some of the regular patients were sensitive enough to detect the pseudopatients and made comments to them like, "You're not crazy. You're a journalist, or a professor (referring to the continual note-taking). You're checking up on the hospital." The hospital personnel were too biased in their views to have any suspicion and went as far as interpreting the note-taking of the pseudopatients as a possible "subset of the compulsive behaviors that are sometimes correlated with schizophrenia."

The most striking experience of the pseudopatients was one of intense depersonalization. The hospital attendants spent only 11 percent of their working day in contact with the patients and most of this time involved nonsocial functions such as work supervision and household chores. The average amount of contact that patients had with staff members per day was 6.8 minutes. During the course of their "hospitalization" the pseudopatients made 185 attemtps to talk with one of the psychiatrists. In 71 percent of the cases, the psychiatrist walked away with no eye contact. In 23 percent of the cases the psychiatrist made eye contact before walking away. In only 6 percent of the attempts did the psychiatrists actually stop and talk. The encounter between the pseudopatients and psychiatrists commonly had the following bizarre and frustrating form:

"Pardon me, Dr. X. Could you tell me when I am eligible for grounds privileges?"

"Good morning, Dave, how are you today?" (The psychiatrist moves off without waiting for a response.)

Rosenhan and his colleagues came away from their experiences with the following conclusions:

Neither anecdotal nor "hard" data can convey the overwhelming sense of powerlessness which invades the individual as he is continually exposed to the depersonalization of the psychiatric hospital. It hardly matters *which* psychiatric hospital . . .

Powerlessness was evident everywhere. The patient is deprived of many of his legal rights by dint of his psychiatric commitment. He is shorn of credibility by virtue of his psychiatric label. His freedom of movement is restricted. He cannot initiate contact with the staff, but only respond to such overtures as they make. Personal privacy is minimal. Patient quarters and possessions can be entered and examined by any staff member, for whatever reason. His personal history and anguish is available to any staff member (often including the "grey lady" and "candy striper" volunteer) who chooses to read his folder, regardless of their therapeutic relationship to him. His personal hygiene and waste evacuation are often monitored. The water closets may have no doors.

Rosenhan and his colleagues felt that most of the hospital staff were people who really cared about the patients and were committed to their work. The problem, they felt, was that the hospital staff were working under very disadvantageous conditions. First, there is the fear and distrust that all of us are taught to hold toward the mentally ill. The result of this stigma is an avoidance of patients and a tendency to see everything they do and say as abnormal. The second problem is the hierarchical structure of hospitals, which places the psychiatrists and psychologists at the top and out of contact with the remaining staff and patients. Money is always a problem, but tremendous improvement could be made in mental hospitals just by changing values and teaching the staff members to more clearly understand the patients' point of view.[37]

In 1959 John Howard Griffin performed a powerful experiment in racial empathy by taking medication to have his skin turned black and living in the South as a black man. Among the numerous incidents of maltreatment and dehumanization Griffin experienced was a continual preoccupation of white people with the black sexual stereotype. When Griffin was hitchhiking, white men who picked him up made comments such as:

"Now, don't try to kid me. I wasn't born yesterday. You know you've done such-and-such, just like I have. . . . Tell me, did you ever get a white woman?"

"I understand you make more of an art—or maybe *hobby* out of your sex than we do."

"Well, you people don't seem to have the inhibitions we have. We're all basically puritans. I understand Negroes do a lot more things—different kinds of sex—than we do."

The hypocrisy of whites is shown further by other typical comments:

"We'll sure as hell screw your women. Other than that, you're just *completely off the record as far as we're concerned*. And the quicker you people get that through your heads, the better off you'll be."

"We figure we're doing you people a favor to get some white blood in your kids." [38]

In 1968 Grace Halsell repeated Griffin's study of racial empathy by having her skin blackened and living in Harlem and Mississippi. Things had not changed very much in ten years. At one point, Halsell went into the office of a small store in Mississippi and asked a white woman behind the desk if she could use the phone.

"Git her out of here! . . . We *told* you you're not supposed to be in here!"

Halsell was persistent. Finally, the white woman gave in.

"What's your name, girl?"

The thought raced through Halsell's mind:

But why won't she hand me the phone? Will my black hand on the instrument leave so much blackness that it will rub off on her? Will I never be allowed to touch what she touches? Does my very presence contaminate the air she breathes?

"But hand me the phone," I say, in my usual tone of voice, which is low and quiet, but now controlled by a determined effort. "I speak English. I am able to give my own message."

"Why you *black bitch!*" She screams. . . . "You think you can come in here, tell me how to run my business!"

"If you don't git out of here *this instant,*" the white woman screams, "I'll call the police."

"Yes," I say, in a voice I hardly know. "You do that."

She dials the police, screams into the instrument, "A Nigra in here causing a disturbance!"

A siren is heard and the police arrive.

"This here uppity Nigra," the white woman screams, "causing a commotion. . . . Thinks she can just take over the place, wouldn't stay over there . . . where she belongs."

This time, in the process of being arrested, Halsell is rescued by a Catholic priest.

The same preoccupation with sex, on the part of whites, that Griffin reported was experienced by Halsell. A black woman working in a white home is commonly subjected to sexual advances by the man. Black women on the street receive sexual harassment from whites. After one incident in which Halsell fought off the white man of a house where she was a maid, she asked herself: "What if I were black? What if I had children to support? Could I afford to flee a white man without being paid? What could I tell my husband? Who would believe that a white man tried to rape a black woman?" [39]

A group of students at the University of Illinois attempted to view the world from the perspective of disabled people by spending a day in a wheelchair. The experiences they had as they wheeled themselves around campus, up hills and in and out of elevators, were enlightening:

The looks that I received were very interesting and were consistently the same. People look out of the corner of their eyes and then a downward glance past my legs. They seemed a bit embarrassed.

I am surprised what effect this had on me. I was alone the entire time. I saw no one that I knew, so perhaps this made me take it all very seriously. All I know is that my eyes filled up with tears coming back up alone in that elevator.

As a test of empathy, the role-playing students were asked to give their attitudes toward having a professor in a wheelchair as their supervisor and about spending school funds on facilities for disabled students. Compared with non-participating students, their attitudes were significantly more favorable. Four months after their experience, the role-playing students still had more favorability and tolerance for disabled people than students who had not viewed the world from a wheelchair.[40]

Farley Mowat has written a delightful account of his experiences living among the wolves in northern Canada. During his studies of the wolves' diet, which consisted largely of mice, it occurred to Mowat that in order to fully understand it he should try it himself:

It was imperative for me to prove that a diet of small rodents would suffice to maintain a large carnivore in good condition.

Eating these small mammals presented something of a problem at first because of the numerous minute bones; however I found that the bones could be chewed and swallowed without much difficulty.

During the first week of the mouse diet I found that my vigor remained unimpaired, and that I suffered no apparent ill effects. However, I did begin to develop a craving for fats. It was this which made me realize that my experiment, up to this point, had been rendered partly invalid by an oversight. . . . The wolves, as I should have remembered, *ate the whole mouse*. . . . From this time to the end of the experimental period I too ate the whole mouse, without the skin of course, and I found that my fat craving was considerably eased.

At another point, Mowat made a study of what it was like to stake out the territory of his campsite. Marking his area at intervals of fifteen feet was a chore that took most of the night and numerous trips back to the tent for refueling with tea. Before leaving the wolves, Mowat felt that he should crawl into one of their dens to see what it was like living under the ground. He took his flashlight and wiggled into the entrance tunnel. After squirming for eight feet he ran into the four green eyes of a mother and her pup. A wave of fear raced through Mowat until he realized that he had lived with these wolves all summer. The mother did not growl or attack, but Mowat felt that it was most prudent to make a hasty retreat. His reflections afterward about what he had learned about the wolves, and about himself, by experiencing a piece of their lives are quite moving.[41]

Carl Rogers has pointed out that when other people express an opinion or feeling, we usually don't make an attempt to understand it from their point of view. Instead, we have a tendency to judge or evaluate what they say on the basis of our own perceptions. An example would be when, after leaving a movie, someone says, "Hey, I really liked that movie." Our typical response would be, "Oh yeah? I didn't think it was so hot," or "I liked it too." The point is that we would interpret what the other person said from our own point of view. Rogers suggests that maybe we could first try to appreciate the other person's feelings. Before giving our own evaluation of the movie we could learn more about why the other person felt a certain way. Rogers suggests a simple exercise which you might seriously want to try. The next time you have an argument with somebody, or with a group of people, stop the conversation and institute the following rule. Before anyone can speak, he or she must express the feelings of the person who spoke previously. The previous speaker will then have the chance to say, "Yes, that's what I meant," or "No, what I really meant was . . ." It might also help to have a neutral person as a sort of mediator. You will find that this is much more difficult to do than it sounds. We are more caught up in our own feelings and opinions than we often realize. We are more interested in having people become similar to us than in attempting to understand their point of view and learning how they feel. But try it! Empathy will help to appreciate dissimilarity.[42]

Decreasing Threat. In addition to increasing our empathy we can learn to appreciate dissimilar people by becoming less personally threatened by them. One reason that dissimilar people are threatening to us is because they make us doubt ourselves. We feel that if they are right we must be wrong, and that is bad. It is certainly possible, however, for two people to have different attitudes without one of them being "bad" and the other "good." What aggravates this self-doubt the most is when a person who disagrees with us is dogmatic. A dogmatic person who is dissimilar gives the message that he or she is right and we are wrong. An open-minded person who is dissimilar gives the message that there is room in the world for both of us. Research has shown that dissimilar open-minded people are preferred significantly more than dissimilar dogmatic people.[43]

It might be hard for us to make other people open-minded, but we can at least set a good example. In addition, we can realize that even dogmatic dissimilar people don't make us wrong. We can tolerate them and, in return, they might tolerate us. There are a lot of interesting dissimilar people in the world for us to meet if we can learn to empathize and overcome our negative first impressions.

NOTES

1 P. N. MIDDLEBROOK, *Social Psychology and Modern Life* (New York: Alfred A. Knopf, 1974), Chapter 9.

2 D. BYRNE, *The Attraction Paradigm* (New York: Academic Press, 1971). Much of this chapter is based on the work of Byrne. I highly recommend Byrne's book to readers who wish to learn about research on similarity and attraction in more detail.

3 B. A. SCHILLER, "A Quantative Analysis of Marriage Selection in a Small Group," *Journal of Social Psychology*, 1932, 3, 297–319.

4 D. BYRNE, *op. cit.*, pp. 27–28.

5 D. BYRNE, J. LAMBERTH, and H. E. MITCHELL, "Husband-Wife Similarity in Response to Erotic Stimuli," cited in D. Byrne, *op. cit.*, p. 384.

6 L. M. TERMAN and P. BUTTENWIESER, "Personality Factors in Marital Compatibility: I.," *Journal of Social Psychology*, 1935, 6, 143–171.

7 L. M. TERMAN and P. BUTTENWIESER, "Personality Factors in Marital Compatibility: II," *Journal of Social Psychology*, 1935, 6, 267–289.

8 Z. RUBIN, *Liking and Loving: An Invitation to Social Psychology* (New York: Holt, Rinehart and Winston, 1973), pp. 195–196.

9 A. C. KERKHOFF and K. E. DAVIS, "Value Consensus and Need Complimentarity in Mate Selection," *American Sociological Review*, 1962, 27, 295–303.

10 H. M. RICHARDSON, "Community of Values as a Factor in Friendships of College and Adult Women," *Journal of Social Psychology*, 1940, 11, 303–312.

11 C. N. WINSLOW, "A Study of the Extent of Agreement Between Friends' Opinion and Their Ability to Estimate the Opinions of Each Other," *Journal of Social Psychology*, 1937, 8, 433–442.

12 E. O. LAUMANN, "Friends of Urban Men: An Assessment of Accuracy in Reporting Their Socioeconomic Attributes, Mutual Choice, and Attitude Agreement," *Sociometry*, 1969, 32, 54–69.

13 W. R. BERKOWITZ, J. C. NEBEL, and J. W. REITMAN, "Height and Interpersonal Attraction: The 1969 Mayoral Election in New York City," Paper delivered at the meeting of the American Psychological Association, Washington, D.C., 1971. Cited by Z. Rubin, *op. cit.*, p. 136.

14 S. SCHACHTER, "Deviation, Rejection, and Communication," *Journal of Abnormal and Social Psychology*, 1951, 46, 190–207.

15 D. Byrne, *op. cit.*

16 D. BYRNE, J. LAMBERTH, J. PALMER, and O. LONDON, "Sequential Effects as a Function of Explicit and Implicit Interpolated Attraction Responses," *Journal of Personality and Social Psychology*, 1969, 13, 70–78.

17 D. BYRNE, *op. cit.*, Chapter 6.

18 D. BYRNE, *op. cit.*, pp. 98–101.

19 D. BYRNE, *op. cit.*, Chapter 8.

20 D. W. NOVAK and LERNER, M. J., "Rejection as a Consequence of Perceived Similarity," *Journal of Personality and Social Psychology*, 1968, 9, 147–152. Cited in D. Byrne, *op. cit.*, pp. 134–144.

21 S. E. TAYLOR and D. R. METTEE, "When Similarity Breeds Contempt," *Journal of Personality and Social Psychology*, 1971, 20, 75–81.

22 R. A. BARON, "Behavioral Effects of Interpersonal Attraction: Compliance With the Requests of Liked and Disliked Others." Cited in D. Byrne, *op. cit.,* p. 244.

23 D. BYRNE, "Interpersonal Attraction and Attitude Similarity," *Journal of Abnormal and Social Psychology,* 1961, 62, 713–715.

24 D. BYRNE, M. H. BOND, and M. J. DIAMOND, "Response to Political Candidates as a Function of Attitude Similarity Dissimilarity," *Human Relations,* 1969, 22, 251–262.

25 D. BYRNE, *The Attraction Paradigm,* pp. 258–259.

26 R. E. SMITH, L. SMYTHE, and D. LIEN, "Inhibition of Helping Behavior by Similar and Dissimilar Nonreactive Fellow Bystanders," Unpublished manuscript, University of Washington, 1971. Cited in D. Byrne, *op. cit.,* p. 262.

27 G. L. CLORE and J. B. GORMLY, "Knowing, Feeling, and Liking. A Psychophysiological Study of Attraction," *Journal of Research in Personality,* 1974, 8, 218–230.

28 B. L. MEADOW, "The Effects of Attitude Similarity-Dissimilarity and Enjoyment on the Perception of Time," Unpublished master's thesis, Purdue University, 1971. Cited in D. Byrne, *op. cit.,* p. 310.

29 R. E. SMITH, B. L. MEADOW, and T. K. SISK, "Attitude Similarity, Interpersonal Attraction, and Evaluative Social Perception," *Psychonomic Science,* 1970, 18, 226–227.

30 A. SAPOLSKY, "Effect of Interpersonal Relationships Upon Verbal Conditioning," *Journal of Abnormal and Social Psychology,* 1960, 60, 241–246.

31 D. BYRNE, C. R. ERVIN, and J. LAMBERTH, "Continuity Between the Experimental Study of Attraction and 'Real Life' Computer Dating," *Journal of Personality and Social Psychology,* 1970, 16, 157–165.

32 D. L. MERRITT, "The Relationships Between Qualifications and Attitudes in a Teacher Selection Situation," Unpublished doctoral dissertation, Syracuse University, 1970. Cited in D. Byrne, *op. cit.,* p. 394.

33 W. GRIFFITT and T. JACKSON, "The Influence of Ability and Nonability Information on Personal Selection Decisions," *Psychological Reports,* 1970, 27, 959–962.

34 C. GOLIGHTLY, D. M. HUFFMAN, and D. BYRNE, "Liking and Loaning." Cited in D. Byrne, *op. cit.,* p. 396.

35 P. L. MAHAFFEY, "Attraction Affect as a Cue for Dispensing Positive and Negative Behaviors to a Stranger," Unpublished master's thesis, University of Texas, 1969. Cited in D. Byrne, *op. cit.,* p. 397.

36 W. GRIFFITT and T. JACKSON, "Simulated Jury Decisions: The Influence of Jury-Defendant Attitude Similarity-Dissimilarity." Cited in D. Byrne, *op. cit.,* p. 398.

37 D. L. ROSENHAN, "On Being Sane in Insane Places," *Science,* 1973, 179, 250–258.

38 J. H. GRIFFIN, *Black Like Me* (Boston: Houghton Mifflin, 1961).

39 G. HALSELL, *Soul Sister* (New York: World Publishing Company, 1969).

40 G. L. CLORE and K. M. JEFFREY, "Emotional Role Playing, Attitude Change, and Attraction Toward a Disabled Other," *Journal of Personality and Social Psychology*, 1972, 23, 105–111.

41 F. MOWAT, *Never Cry Wolf* (New York: Dell Publishing Company, 1963).

42 C. R. ROGERS, "Communication: Its Blocking and its Facilitation," Paper presented to the Centennial Conference on Communication, Northwestern University, Evanston, Ill., 1951.

43 L. A. HODGES and D. BYRNE, "Verbal Dogmatism as a Potentiator of Intolerance," *Journal of Personality and Social Psychology*, 1972, 21, 312–317.

8

The Art of Ingratiation

If you were to make a list of the five things that are most important to you, it is very probable that one of them would be to be liked. Dale Carnegie, author of *How To Win Friends And Influence People*, talks about our "gnawing and unfaltering human hunger" for appreciation.[1] The public has responded to Carnegie's suggestions for winning friends by purchasing over seven and a half million copies of his book and keeping it on *The New York Times* best-seller list for an all-time record of ten years.

Research that has been conducted on interpersonal attraction during the forty years since Carnegie's book was published can be used to evaluate and elaborate on the suggestions for winning friends which he originally proposed. The focus of this chapter will be on the ways people have learned to ingratiate themselves with others. The process of ingratiation has been described by Edward E. Jones as the actions in which we engage to make ourselves more attractive to others. Ingratiation differs from flattery in at least two ways. Flattery is used to obtain benefits or goods rather than to increase attractiveness. In addition, flattery is limited to bestowal of overgenerous praise. Ingratiation, on the other hand, involves a variety of different possible strategies.[2] We can now look at these various strategies for getting others to like us and evaluate how they work and when they are most effective.

GIVING POSITIVE EVALUATIONS

We like people who appreciate us. It stands to reason that people will like us if we appreciate them. Research studies have shown, as Dale

Carnegie suggested, that praise can go a long way in increasing how attractive we are to others.

The general method of determining how positive evaluations influence liking has been to expose participants in experiments to evaluations of different kinds from another person. The participants are then assessed on their attitudes and reactions toward that person. It has been found that positive evaluators are liked better than negative evaluators.[3]

Evaluations of Performance. Participants in a study were led to believe they had done very well or very poorly on a test of logic. They were then sent a note by another person which said that they were either the first choice or last choice of that person as a future teammate. Whether or not participants experienced success or failure, they liked the positive note sender significantly more than they liked the negative note sender.[4]

College students participating in another study took a test and were told that an evaluator had either thought they would do very well or very poorly on the test. When asked for their opinions of the evaluators, the students were much more favorable toward an evaluator who had predicted a positive rather than negative outcome for their performance.[5]

Male college students were given the task of conducting five telephone conversations with a female student unknown to them. The students' voices in the telephone conversations were taped and supposedly judged by females at a neighboring college on social skill and grace. Later, the male students listened to a tape-recorded assessment of their social skill which they thought had been made by one of the female evaluators. For some of the males, the female's evaluation was very favorable and accepting. For other males, the female was critical and rejecting. When the males were asked what they thought about the females who did the judging, they expressed significantly more liking for females who had praised rather than criticized them.[6]

Personal Evaluations. Participants in a study were assigned to groups of five or six members and given a series of problems and issues to discuss. After about an hour the groups were interrupted and the participants were asked to rate each other on favorability. The participants were then shown ratings which they had supposedly received from the other group members. Half of the participants were led to believe that they were highly valued by other group members and half of the participants were given information indicating that they were not valued by other group members.

At the end of the study, the participants were asked how much they had enjoyed participating in their group and how willing they would be to return for another discussion in the future. Participants who were given positive evaluations from the other group members expressed much more favorability toward the group and desire to return as compared with participants who had received negative evaluations.[7]

Another study using discussion groups gave participants the expectation that certain group members would like them very much, while other group members would not like them. After a brief discussion, the participants were asked to choose another group member as a partner for a two-person team. Participants were significantly more likely to choose someone who they thought would like them rather than dislike them.[8]

College students were interviewed for ten minutes about their academic interests, political views, and future plans. After the interview they were shown an evaluation that had supposedly been made of them by another student of the same sex who had been observing them. The evaluations were either favorable, communicating liking and compatibility, or unfavorable, with judgments of disliking and incompatibility. Participants then interacted with their evaluator in a two-person game and gave their impressions of the evaluator on a rating form. Students who had previously been rated favorably by the evaluator expressed significantly more liking for the evaluator than students who had been rated unfavorably. In addition, male students were more cooperative with positive evaluators while they were playing the game.[9]

In three other studies, participants were given either positive or negative evaluations by others on attributes ranging from how interesting and informed they were to qualities of friendliness, competence, dependability, and maturity. In all cases, the participants expressed more liking for evaluators who had been favorable toward them rather than evaluators who had been unfavorable.[10,11,12]

JUDGING THE SINCERITY OF PRAISE

People thrive on positive evaluation and if there is any way for them to convince themselves that a compliment is true they will do so. Research has shown that people who don't see certain positive attributes in themselves will still be very much drawn to someone else who says they are there. The only exception would be when there is strong external evidence that the particular positive attributes don't exist.[13] Dale Carnegie was right. Praise can go a long way. However, we all know that in order for praise to win friends it has to be interpreted as sincere. Dale Carnegie was adamant about this:[14]

> No! No! No! I am not suggesting flattery! Far from it. . . . The difference between appreciation and flattery? That is simple. One is sincere and the other insincere. One comes from the heart out; the other from the teeth out. One is unselfish; the other is universally condemned.

We have all learned, in one way or another, how to judge when people are being sincere or insincere in their praise. One of the advantages of scientific research on first impressions is that it helps us to outline in a fairly specific manner the various methods that we use to make these judgments of sincerity. Let us look at what research studies have found about how we determine when compliments are sincere and when they are insincere.

Compliments Must Be Believable. It is obvious that compliments have to be plausible before they will succeed in getting someone to like us. Compliments that are not believable will be received in a negative way and give the person reason to dislike us.

Employees at a telephone company were divided into teams of four and given several problems to solve. Team members worked individually on the problems, with the understanding that their individual scores would be combined into a total score to determine which team would win. Some employees were led to believe that they had done very well on the problems and had helped their team to win. Other employees were told that they had done poorly on the problems and had caused their team to lose. After the contest was over the group members read a note that had supposedly been sent to them by one of their teammates. Half of the participants received positive notes stating that the note sender would very much like to have them on the same team in the future. The remaining participants received negative notes in which the note sender expressed the desire not to be on the same team again.

It is not surprising that participants who had done well and helped their team win preferred note senders who were positive rather than negative. When you think about it, it is also not surprising that the participants who had done poorly and caused their team to lose were very negative toward the positive note senders. It seemed just too far-fetched for employees to tell someone who had caused their team to lose that they would still like to be on the same team in the future. The positive notes to teammates who did poorly were especially unbelievable because there had been no social interaction involved and the only important basis on which to choose team members would have been their performance on the tasks.[15]

Another study testing the plausibility of praise had college students perform a simulated game in which they acted as air controllers and made a series of critical decisions. Four other students observed the participants as they played the game and gave evaluations about how competent they thought their performance had been. When three evaluators gave average evaluations and one evaluator gave a very positive evaluation, the participants showed least liking for the highly positive evaluator. Apparently, the highly positive evalution was too far from the participants' sense of reality to be taken seriously.[16]

Participants in a third study were given the task of making an argument in favor of an issue with which they strongly agreed or strongly disagreed. Half of the participants were given feedback indicating that their performance had been very good. The remaining participants were led to believe that their performance had been quite poor. After getting this rather clear indication about how well they had performed, the participants were given different evaluations from people who had observed them during their arguments.

Again, it is not surprising that participants who felt they had performed well were very favorable toward people who gave them positive evaluations. When participants thought their performance had been poor, they were not particularly favorable toward people who evaluated them positively. Participants were especially negative in their feelings when they had done poorly and an evaluator with opposite views from their own gave them a positive evaluation. It seems unpleasantly condescending, when you know you have done poorly, for someone who disagrees with you still to give you a positive evaluation.[17]

One way to make compliments more believable is to get the message across that you are discriminating and don't give compliments to just anybody. This can be at least partially accomplished by giving compliments that specifically apply to the person in question rather than compliments that are very general and true for everyone. It is also probably better not to give blindly positive evaluations, but rather to mix at least a few neutral or mildly negative evaluations along with the positive ones.

Female students received evaluations from a male student that were either favorable or unfavorable. The favorable evaluator said that he liked the female and thought she was friendly, intelligent, and competent. The unfavorable evaluator said that he did not like the female and felt that she was unfriendly, unintelligent, and not competent. Half of the females were given the impression that the male evaluator was very discerning in his judgments. They watched the male make ratings of paintings on a rating scale and saw that he was confident and discriminating enough to use both positive and negative poles of the scale. The remaining females were led to believe the male evaluator was not very discriminating and somewhat wishy-washy. The male they watched always stuck to the middle of the scale when rating the paintings.

It is not unexpected that females liked the male better when he gave favorable rather than unfavorable evaluations. In addition, whether or not the evaluations were favorable or unfavorable, the females liked the male much more when he was discriminating. We like to be praised, but we especially like people who praise us when we feel they are discriminating.[18]

Looking for Ulterior Motives. In judging whether or not a compliment is sincere we make some determination about its believability. We also look to see whether the person making it is dependent upon us for one thing or another. We are much less likely to take a compliment seriously when it comes from someone who has something to gain by winning our favor.

College students revealed some things about themselves in an interview and were observed through a one-way mirror by an evaluator. The evaluator either gave negative evaluations, average evaluations that corresponded with the participants' self-concepts, or very positive evaluations that were more favorable than the participants' self-concepts. When participants believed that the evaluator was motivated to be accurate and objective, they liked the most positive evaluator the best. When the participants thought that the evaluator might want to ask them a favor after the study, they liked the average evaluator the best.[19]

Participants in a similar study were interviewed and evaluated by an observer who had watched the interview through a one-way mirror. The observer either gave very favorable or very unfavorable evaluations. Half of the participants thought that the observer had no ulterior motives and was being objective. The remaining participants were under the impression that the observer was trying to win their approval. When the evaluations were favorable, participants liked the observer with no ulterior motives significantly more than the observer with ulterior motives. When the evaluations were unfavorable, participants preferred the observer who had ulterior motives. This last finding is interesting because it involves a situation in which a person is trying to win someone else's approval by being derogatory. If we receive negative evaluations from someone who is trying to win our approval, we can ignore them and save our self-esteem much more easily than if we are evaluated negatively by someone who is being objective.[20]

When college students were asked to judge a student who had insulted his friend, they were less rejecting if the student who did the insulting had good intentions. It was more acceptable if the student insulted his friend to get him to study harder than if he insulted his friend to make a good impression on his professor.[21]

One fairly effective way to minimize the suspicion that we have ulterior motives is to have praise delivered by a "disinterested" third party. If people hear our praise through someone else, they are less likely to think we are trying to get something out of them. Another way to minimize the perception of ulterior motives is to arrange it so the person in question "overhears" our praise while we are speaking to another person.

Participants in a study were placed in situations in which they could listen to conversations that other people were having about issues of contemporary interest. In some cases it was made clear that the people who were talking were aware of the participants listening to them. In other cases the participants were led to believe they were listening to the conversations without the people's knowledge. Participants were much more influenced by the opinions the people were expressing when the people were supposedly unaware of their presence.[22]

We have discussed a number of studies showing that positive evaluators are preferred over negative evaluators. A crucial feature of these studies was that the evaluators supposedly believed that the evaluations were not going to be made public. If someone gives you a positive evaluation, believing that you will never see it, you are likely to take that positive evaluation very seriously. If someone evaluates you positively, knowing you will learn of the evaluation, there is some ambiguity. Before taking the evaluation seriously, you have to rule out ulterior motives.

Up to this point, we can conclude that positive evaluators are liked more than negative evaluators and that positive evaluators are liked best if they are believable and not guided by ulterior motives. Compliments are more likely to appear sincere and free of ulterior motives if the evaluator has nothing obvious to gain and supposedly is not aware that the evaluation will become known.

Another method for making compliments effective, which was briefly mentioned earlier, is strategically to mix neutral or mildly negative evaluations with praise. Edward E. Jones has described this approach as concocting "a judicious blend of the bitter and the sweet." [23]

Mixing the Bitter with the Sweet. A mixture of neutral or mildly negative evaluations with praise can function to make the praise more effective in at least two ways. We have already learned that an evaluator is more likely to be favored if he or she seems discerning. Certainly a blindly positive evaluator will not come across as discriminating as an evaluator who uses some qualifications in bestowing praise. A bitter-sweet mixture can also strengthen praise by raising a small amount of anxiety and self-doubt in a person which then can be favorably and pleasantly relieved. This is done by giving negative evaluations to a person at first and then switching to positive evaluations over a period of time.

Participants in a study were placed in a situation in which they "overheard" another person make evaluations about them to the experimenter. In one case, the evaluator made favorable comments about the participants from the beginning and continued to be favorable throughout the study. In another case, the evaluator started out by saying negative things about the participants, but then slowly changed until the evaluations ended up as positive.

When participants were asked for their reactions to the evaluators they expressed significantly more liking for the evaluator who switched from negative to positive evaluations than they did for the evaluator who was consistently positive. Another part of the study found that an evaluator who was originally favorable and became unfavorable was liked less than an evaluator who was always unfavorable. Apparently, having someone's favor and losing it is worse than never having it at all. Not having someone's favor and winning it is sweeter than having it all along.[24]

The tendency for changing or contrasting evaluations to have more influence than consistent evaluations has some important implications. A husband and wife who have been happy over a long period of time might not be particularly affected by praise from each other. A compliment from a stranger, on the other hand, could be unexpected and therefore have a stronger impact than the same compliment from the spouse. In the same vein, a husband and wife who are used to sharing a positive relationship may be very adversely affected by negative comments from one to the other. In this case, a negative comment from a stranger would be less of a contrast and less influential than the same criticism from a spouse.[25]

Other implications of changing versus consistent responses from others have been found in research studies. It was shown in one study, for example, that children were more influenced by praise from strangers than by praise from their own parents. This is probably because children are used to attention from their parents, but attention from strangers is something new and different.[26] A second study found that people react more positively when another person agrees after first disagreeing with them, compared with instances in which the other person agrees with them from the beginning.[27]

Participants in a third study received information from strangers which either agreed or disagreed with their attitudes on matters of current interest. In one case, participants were exposed to three people who disagreed with them and then to someone who agreed with them. In another case, participants received agreement from someone after being agreed with on three previous occasions. Participants who had experienced disagreement were significantly more favorable toward someone who finally agreed with them than participants who had experienced agreement all of the time. In addition, participants who experienced continual agreement had a tendency to diminish their liking for successive others who agreed with them. We need to be shaken from our complacency from time to time to appreciate positive reactions from others.[28]

It may have occurred to you that being changeable rather than consistent in positive responses is very much like the age-old game of playing hard to get. Over 2,000 years ago, Socrates made the following suggestion to a prostitute named Theodota:

They will appreciate your favors most highly if you wait till they ask for them. The sweetest meats, you see, if served before they are wanted seem sour, and to those who had enough they are positively nauseating; but even poor fare is very welcome when offered to a hungry man. (Theodota inquired) And how can I make them hungry for my fare? (Socrates' reply) Why, in the first place, you must not offer it to them when they have had enough—but prompt them by behaving as a model of Propriety, by a show of reluctance to yield, and by holding back until they are as keen as can be; and then the same gifts are much more to the recipient than when they're offered before they are desired.[29]

Ovid, the Roman poet, offered similar advice:

Fool, if you feel no need to guard your girl for her own sake, see that you guard her for mine, so I may want her the more. Easy things nobody wants, but what is forbidden is tempting. . . . Anyone who can love the wife of an indolent cuckold, I should suppose, would steal buckets of sand from the shore.[30]

What does research say about playing hard to get? Elaine Walster and her colleagues conducted a series of studies to find an answer. In one study, male students were given the telephone number of a computer date and when they called her she either eagerly accepted their offer or played hard to get. When playing hard to get, the female said that she had met quite a few people since signing up for computer dating and was pretty busy all week. Finally, after some hesitation, the hard-to-get female also accepted the date. When the men were contacted after their dates and asked to evaluate the females, whether or not the females had played hard to get made very little difference.

In a second study, Walster and her colleagues enlisted the help of a prostitute and arranged it so that she would act normally toward some customers and play hard to get for others. When playing hard to get the prostitute said, "Just because I see you this time it doesn't mean that you can have my phone number or see me again. I'm going to start school soon, so I won't have much time, so I'll only be able to see the people that I like the best." In this case, when the woman played hard to get, men appeared to like her less and they were less likely to call her again in the future.

The studies we have just looked at did not support the strategy of playing hard to get and prompted Walster and her colleagues to do some serious thinking. After carefully interviewing a group of men about their feelings toward hard-to-get and easy-to-get women it became clear that one of the problems with hard-to-get women is that they raise considerable self-doubt in men. A woman who comes across as too hard to get may threaten a man and make him lose his confidence. This insight led to a third study.

Male students who signed up for computer dating were exposed to three different kinds of women. Some of the women came across as hard to get for all men. Other women appeared easy to get for all men. A third group of women indicated that they were generally hard to get, but they were willing to make themselves available to the student in question. The last group of women was overwhelmingly preferred. Women who are easy to get for everyone appear to be nonselective and unpopular. Women who are hard to get for everyone give the impression of being unfriendly, cold, and rigid. The woman who is generally hard to get, but willing to make herself available to the man in question, has the qualities (at least to that man) of being selective and popular, and also offers the promise of being friendly, warm, and easy to get along with.[31]

CONFORMING AND AGREEING WITH OTHERS

We learned in Chapter 7 how much people prefer others who are similar rather than dissimilar. Certainly, an effective way to ingratiate ourselves with another person is to appear similar by conforming in our attitudes and behavior. As with giving compliments, of course, our attempts to ingratiate ourselves by conforming and agreeing must be believable and interpreted as sincere. The rules that we learned in the previous section for giving praise also hold for showing similarity.

One way to make conformity believable and to minimize the suspicion of ulterior motives is to show agreement with people before they express their own opinions. If we state an opinion and someone else then agrees with us, we don't know if that person is really sincere or is just agreeing to make a good impression. On the other hand, if someone else states an opinion which agrees with ours before we have made our view known, we would more than likely interpret their similarity as real. The trick is to find out the opinions of others without their knowledge and then to demonstrate similarity in a way that appears spontaneous. This was shown in a study in which participants listened to a conversation between two people, one of whom always agreed very closely with the other. In half of the cases, the agreeing person always spoke first. In the other cases, the agreeing person spoke after hearing the opinions of the other. When the participants gave evaluations of the agreeing person they were significantly more favorable when the agreeing person had spoken first. The agreeing person who spoke after hearing the other person was viewed as manipulative and insincere.[32]

Another way to make conformity believable is to use the bitter-sweet strategy by mixing disagreement with agreement. Ingratiation is most effective when you agree with people on important issues and disagree with them on unimportant issues.[33] The hard-to-get strategy can also be implemented by showing disagreement with another person at first and slowly moving to agreement over time.

Participants in a study interacted with another person who either agreed with them, disagreed with them, or disagreed at first and then agreed. The person who disagreed at first and then yielded to the opinions of the participants was liked more than the person who agreed with the participants all of the time. The person who disagreed all of the time was liked the least. In addition to liking a person who yielded better than a person who always agreed, participants also found that person more reinforcing. Participants were more inclined to make their opinions known to a person who disagreed at first and then yielded than to a person who always agreed. Participants were much slower to make their opinions known to someone who always disagreed.[34]

PRESENTING A FAVORABLE IMAGE

If we wanted to get someone else to like us we would naturally be inclined to present a favorable image and make ourselves appear valuable to that person. As long as the person has no reason to doubt us, presenting a good image is a straightforward strategy for ingratiation.

Students who were going to be interviewed were either motivated to get an interviewer to like them or not to care about what the interviewer thought of them. It was made clear that the interviewer would have no reason to suspect what they said and would never be in a position to check on the accuracy of their statements. Under these circumstances, the students described themselves to the interviewer in much more glowing terms when they were trying to be liked than when they did not care if they were liked or not.[35]

In most cases, when we are meeting people we tend to be skeptical if they make themselves look too good. Because of our skepticism, we often prefer people who present themselves in a more modest fashion. It has been suggested that people with low status or ability have less leeway in choosing between self-enhancing and self-deprecating strategies for ingratiation than people with high status or ability. People with low status who come on too strongly are especially likely to be seen as trying to prove something, while people with low status who deprecate themselves cause others to be uncomfortable and embarrassed.[36]

High-status and low-status ROTC students were placed in a position in which they were either motivated to make a good impression on others or were not concerned with making a good or a bad impression. When trying to make a good impression, high-status students deprecated themselves quite a bit on unimportant qualities and a small amount on important qualities. The high-status students who wanted to be liked could afford to be very modest on unimportant traits to show that they were approachable and slightly modest on important traits to maintain their respect. Low-status students who were trying to make a good impression could not afford the strategy of being modest. Their main concern was to minimize their weaknesses, especially on unimportant traits. Coming on too strongly on important traits might have been going too far.[37]

The above research suggests that if you are good, and people know it, modesty can be a successful tactic for ingratiation. If you are average or poor, other strategies for ingratiation are better advised. This principle has also been shown in a somewhat different way.

Participants in a study were asked to observe a videotape of a student purportedly trying out for the College Bowl quiz team. In one case the student was obviously of superior ability and in a second case the student was of average ability. Half of the participants saw a videotape in which the superior or average student committed a pratfall by clumsily spilling a cup of coffee all over himself. For the other participants the superior and average students ended the interview without incident. The results of the study were interesting because they showed that the average student was liked less if he committed a blunder, but that the superior student was liked more if he blundered. It was concluded that a superior person who commits a blunder is liked more because by doing so he proves that he is human. An average or mediocre person who blunders only proves that he is clumsy.[38]

Other research has indicated that the extent to which we derogate or are attracted to a person who commits a blunder may also depend on our own self-esteem. It is most likely that people with average self-esteem will come to like a superior person who blunders. If we have very high self-esteem we may prefer a superior person who does not blunder because we don't need the assurance that the person is human. If we have very low self-esteem we may prefer a superior person who does not blunder because we need someone to admire. If we have average or high self-esteem we will probably feel unfavorably toward an average person who blunders. If we have low self-esteem we may identify with the average person who blunders and not wish to react in a derogatory manner.[39]

DECREASING PERSONAL DISTANCE
THROUGH IMMEDIACY

When we meet people for the first time we have a tendency to put up our guard for a while until we get to know them better. We also become sensitive to people at first meeting to see how they will react toward us. It usually doesn't take long to make a judgment on whether or not another person is going to open up a bit or remain distant. We have learned about many of the cues that we use to judge the distance or closeness other people are maintaining as they relate to us. We become sensitive to people's gaze, their physical distance, their body postures and gestures, their facial expressions, and their tone of voice. We also make discriminations about how close of distant people are in what they say and in the words they use to communicate with us. For example, if someone says, "*You and I* did such-and-such," there is not as much closeness as there would be if the person had said, "*We* did such-and-such." The statement, "We *should* get together" does not communicate as much closeness as the statement "We *will* get together."

Morton Wiener and Albert Mehrabian have devised a system for scoring the amount of closeness or distance in verbal statements. They define the amount of closeness or distance between a speaker and the content of his or her communication in terms of *immediacy*. Statements with high immediacy are felt by Wiener and Mehrabian to reflect closeness and positive affect. Statements low in immediacy indicate avoidance and negative affect. Wiener and Mehrabian's system for scoring the immediacy in statements is somewhat complex, but a few examples will give a basic idea of how it works. Statements that separate the speaker from the content of the communication in distance or time are less immediate than statements that do not. Saying "*Those* people need help" is less immediate than saying "*These* people need help." The statement "We *have had* a good relationship" is less immediate than "We *are having* a good relationship." A speaker who refers to the specific object in a communication is more immediate than a speaker who refers to the object indirectly. It is more immediate to say, "I like *John*" rather than to say, "I like *him*." Being passive toward an object is less immediate than being active. It is more immediate to say, "I *want* to see Mary" than it is to say, "I *have* to see Mary." Stating personal feelings in the first person is more immediate than presenting them in the abstract. "*I* think it will work" is more immediate than "*You'd* think it will work" or "*One* would think it will work." [40]

Two different kinds of research studies have been conducted to test the interaction between immediacy and first impressions. One approach has been to take people with different kinds of relationships and measure the amount of immediacy in their communications. A second method is to manipulate the amount of immediacy in a communication and see what effect this has on people's impressions of each other.

Measuring Immediacy in Communications. College students who favored Eisenhower for president and college students who favored Stevenson for president were asked to discuss the topic "Who should be elected to the presidency and why?" When students argued in favor of their preferred candidate they used the "I" significantly more often than when they argued for the candidate they did not prefer.[41]

Participants in two different studies were given several tasks to perform involving reading and comprehension or concept formation. It was arranged that participants would think they had failed on some of the tasks and succeeded on others. The people were then asked to write a statement about each of the tasks they had attempted. The statements written about the success-associated tasks had significantly more immediacy than the statements written about the tasks associated with failure.[42,43]

People were asked to think of a person they liked and write a sentence or two about themselves and the liked person. They were also asked to think of a person they disliked and write a sentence or two about themselves and the disliked person. When these statements were scored, there was significantly more immediacy in the sentences involving liked rather than disliked persons.[44] Participants in a similar study were asked to write either a positive or a negative statement about someone they liked or disliked. The positive statements about the liked people had the highest immediacy and the negative statements about the disliked people had the lowest immediacy.[45]

A positive relationship has also been found between immediacy and liking in spoken communication. People were asked to say a few words about someone they liked and someone they disliked. Statements about liked persons had significantly more immediacy than statements about disliked persons.[46]

Immediacy in communication appears to be related to liking in a linear manner. With more liking there is more immediacy, with less liking there is less immediacy.[47]

A simpler way to measure immediacy is to count the number of words communicated by a speaker about another person. Participants in a study were asked to write letters of recommendation for someone they either liked or disliked. The letters written for liked people were significantly longer than the letters written for disliked people. When given specific qualifications or personal attributes to discuss in the letters, the participants went into much more detail when they wrote letters for people they liked rather than disliked.[48]

Manipulating Immediacy in Communication. People were given statements that had supposedly been made by two different speakers about another person and were asked to judge the speaker's attitudes toward that person. One of the speakers made statements with high immediacy. Some examples are, "I know X," "I visited X," "I saw X." The second speaker had expressed statements with low immediacy, such as, "Our group knows X," "I visited X's house," "I saw X's car." Results showed that the immediate speaker was seen as liking the person spoken about significantly more than the nonimmediate speaker.[49]

A similar study had people judge statements in which immediacy was varied along several different dimensions. Some of the dimensions of immediacy included were separation between speaker and object in distance or time, activity-passivity, and reciprocity. Examples of statements with high immediacy are "I've seen this clerk before," "Mike is showing me his house," "I'm going to write a letter to Joe," "Dave and I go for rides." Statements with low immediacy included "I've seen that clerk before," "Mike showed me his house," "I have to write a letter to Joe," "I go for rides with Dave." People making the judgments felt that the immediate speaker liked the person who was being talked about significantly more than did the nonimmediate speaker.[50]

Using People's Names. Decreasing the distance between yourself and others by speaking in more immediate terms is a rather subtle means of ingratiation. The tests that we learned earlier for sincerity are less likely to be involved here because people are probably not so aware of the different ways in which immediacy in communication can be varied. Another more direct way to increase immediacy in verbal communication is to call other people by their names. Dale Carnegie has proposed using people's names as one of his six rules for getting them to like you. Because being called by name is something that we are aware of, tests for the sincerity of name-users have to be taken seriously. The most relevant test for sincerity when someone uses your name is whether or not the person has something to gain by winning your favor.

People were asked to listen to tape recordings of job interviews and give their impressions of the person who was being interviewed for the job. In some of the interviews the job applicant used the interviewer's name (Mr. So-and-so) six times and in some of the interviews the job applicants did not use the interviewer's name. The interviews were about five minutes long. In this study, job applicants who used the interviewer's name were rated significantly more insincere, incompetent, and phony, as compared with job applicants who did not call the interviewer by name. In addition, the people listening to the interviews stated that they liked the name-using applicants significantly less and would be significantly less willing to hire them.[51]

In a similar study, in which people looked at videotapes of job interviews, an *interviewer* who used the job applicant's name was rated as significantly friendlier and warmer than an interviewer who did not. Interestingly enough, the job applicant was also rated as more friendly, warm, and competent when he was called by name.[52]

There are two conclusions that can be drawn here. First, because a job applicant has ulterior motives and is dependent upon an interviewer's approval, he is rated very negatively when he uses the interviewer's name. An interviewer, on the other hand, is not dependent on the job applicant's approval and is thus rated favorably when he uses the applicant's name. A second conclusion from this research is that a job applicant who is called by name is rated more favorably than a job applicant who is not called by name. Presumably, the behavior of a person with prestige can serve as a model for our attitudes toward others.

Another example in which calling a person by name was reacted to in a favorable manner involved a situation in which a female college student interviewed a group of male students about their attitudes on various issues of contemporary interest. Two males were interviewed at the same time. The interviewer called one of the males by name eleven times during the interview and used the other male's name only once. In all other respects, such as eye contact, tone of voice, body posture, and order of questioning, the interviewer treated both males exactly the same. When the interview was over, the males were asked for their reactions. Both the males who were called by name and the males who were not called by name felt that the interviewer had most liked the male whose name she had used. Males who were called by name liked the interviewer significantly more than males who were not called by name. In this situation, where the interviewer presumably has no ulterior motives, it is favorable and acceptable if she uses the interviewees' names.[53]

A different kind of study testing for sincerity in use of names involved a situation in which male and female college students were introduced and left alone for fifteen minutes to get to know each other and talk about anything they chose. Immediately before their introduction, half of the males were asked to call the female they met by name at least six times during their conversation. The other males were asked not to use the female's names during their conversation. The females, of course, were not aware of this instruction. After the conversations, the participants evaluated each other on a rating form. Males who had called the females by name were rated by the females as significantly more phony, distant, and trying to make a good impression than males who had not used the females' names. Again, we have a situation in which use of name is evaluated unfavorably when the name-user is in a position of trying to win someone else's favor.[54]

People looking at videotaped interviews of a man and a woman who were supposedly engaged tended to be more unfavorable toward the couple when they used each other's names than when they did not. In this case, the name-using couple did not have anything obvious to gain. They were probably rated in a negative manner because it is unusual for people in our culture to call each other by name. When couples in the interview used each other's names they probably came across as a little unusual or strange.[55]

DECREASING PERSONAL DISTANCE THROUGH SELF-DISCLOSURE

One way to ingratiate ourselves with others is to show them that we trust them and are willing to relate with them on a personal rather than superficial basis. By disclosing personal things about ourselves we can increase the amount of intimacy we share with them and also give them a chance to reciprocate by disclosing more about themselves to us.

Self-Disclosure and Liking. Females were asked how they would feel about meeting another female for the first time who was willing to disclose a little bit, a medium amount, or a large amount about herself. A female who was willing only to talk about low self-disclosing issues such as favorite TV programs and where she went on vacation was not liked very much. A female who wanted at first meeting to talk about very highly disclosing topics, such as birth-control techniques and serious personal problems, was also not liked very much. The most preferred female was one who expressed interest in issues of medium self-disclosure, such as things she enjoyed most in life, and issues worrisome or important to her.[56]

Participants in two different studies were introduced to each other for ten minutes. After indicating in private how much they liked each other they were placed in a situation in which they could talk, choosing whether their messages would be low, medium, or high in self-disclosure. Participants were willing to disclose significantly more about themselves to people they liked than to people they disliked. Participants also liked others most when they disclosed a relatively large amount about themselves and least when they disclosed very little about themselves.[57,58]

Research studies show that we like people who disclose themselves to us more than we like people who do not. The only exception would be if people go overboard and disclose far more about themselves than is appropriate for the situation. People who disclose too much about themselves make us feel uncomfortable. We also feel uncomfortable if people we have just met disclose personal things that are somewhat deviant.

Participants in a study were introduced to a female who disclosed that she had been caught by her mother in a sexual encounter with someone who was either of the same or opposite sex. In both cases, the female was being highly self-disclosing, but she was liked significantly less in the first case, in which her self-disclosure was about something typically thought of as deviant. It's all right to tell a stranger that you were caught in bed with someone of the opposite sex, but telling a stranger you were caught in bed with someone of the same sex is, at least in our present society, going a bit too far![59]

Self-Disclosure and Reciprocity. Research has shown fairly generally that the more we disclose about ourselves to others, the more they will disclose about themselves to us.[60] This rule of reciprocity will hold true unless people go beyond the limit and disclose more than is appropriate for the situation.

A group of college students conducted a study by going into an airport and asking people for a handwriting sample. The students were more interested in *what* the people would write than in their handwriting, but they did not make this known. In order to give some sort of example, the students always wrote a short "handwriting sample" for the people to see before the people wrote theirs. For one-third of the people, the samples written by the students were highly self-disclosing:

. . . Lately I've been thinking about how I really feel about myself. I think that I'm pretty well adjusted, but I occasionally have some questions about my sexual adequacy.

For another third of the people the students wrote samples that were very low in self-disclosure:

. . . Right now I'm in the process of collecting handwriting samples for a school project. I think I will stay here for a while longer, and then call it a day.

The remaining people saw handwriting samples that were average in self-disclosure. In one case, the students looked as if they were being very personal in the handwriting samples they wrote. They thought a moment, looked up at the ceiling, and then wrote the sample as if they were doing it specifically for that one person. In this condition, an interesting thing happened. When the students wrote a very low self-disclosing handwriting sample the people who were approached also wrote a sample that was low in self-disclosure. The people who saw a sample that was medium in self-disclosure disclosed a great deal about themselves. When the students wrote a sample that was very high in self-disclosure the people reversed themselves. They again did not disclose very much about themselves. Apparently, writing such a highly self-disclosing message to people who were strangers was inappropriate and made them feel uncomfortable.

In a second condition of the study, the students wrote their handwriting samples under a very different set of circumstances. They made it obvious that they were copying the message from a piece of paper. The sample they wrote was not personal and did not come from them. In this condition, the people who were approached did not feel so uncomfortable about reading a very highly self-disclosing message because it was not personal, and they reciprocated by writing a highly self-disclosing message in return.

Another interesting point that came out in this study is something that you've probably experienced yourself. People will often disclose a lot more to a stranger than to someone they know. There is less fear from strangers about later embarrassment because we probably won't ever see them again.[61]

SHOWING INTEREST IN PEOPLE

One of the most important suggestions given by Dale Carnegie for getting people to like you is to be a good listener and show interest in what is important to them. There hasn't been much research on this particular way of ingratiating yourself with others, but some of the examples and anecdotes Carnegie gives may be interesting for you to explore:

Remember that the man you are talking to is a hundred times more interested in himself and his wants and his problems than he is in you and your problems. His toothache means more to him than a famine in China that kills a million people. A boil on his neck interests him more than forty earthquakes in Africa. Think of that the next time you start a conversation.[62]

Carnegie describes how Theodore Roosevelt would sit up late at night to read about whatever subjects were important to the people he would meet with the next day. When Dorothy Dix interviewed a celebrated bigamist about his secret for making women fall in love with him, he said it was no trick at all; all you had to do was talk to a woman about herself.[63]

WHERE DO WE GO FROM HERE?

One of the things which people often complain about when asking psychologists questions is their tendency to respond with the answer, "It depends." Throughout this book we have explored a vast array of factors which influence first impressions between people as they encounter one another. After learning about hundreds of studies with many interesting findings, we come away with very few general rules or laws for predicting how people will respond to each other when they first meet. There is no need for this to bother you. After all, people are very complex. The situations in which people interact are also complex. It shouldn't be surprising that it is beyond the scope of our present knowledge to develop laws of behavior which can take all of these complexities into consideration. It is premature and probably inappropriate to make conclusions about the meaning of every sitting position, facial expression, or eye blink which people make.

What we have come away with is a scientific framework with which we can continue our interest and awareness of first impressions. We have learned about the two general ways in which psychologists study variables influencing first impressions. In one kind of study, variables such as gaze, facial expressions, and tone of voice are manipulated in controlled situations and the effects of these variables on people are measured. In a second kind of study, the situations or relationships in which people are placed are manipulated and the particular variables of interest are measured.

Our orientation is not toward looking at other people to find a meaning for everything they do. Rather, what we want to do is continue to be curious and introspective. You will find that your encounters with other people will be more interesting now because you are aware of many different factors which influence first impressions. You may not have all of the answers at this point, but you likely have many questions. Your interest in first impressions is just beginning. It is time now to go out, look, become aware, and remain open-minded.

NOTES

1 D. CARNEGIE, *How to Win Friends and Influence People* (New York: Pocket Books, 1972), p. 31.

2 E. E. JONES, *Ingratiation: A Social Psychological Analysis* (New York: Appleton-Century-Crofts, 1964), p. 2.

3 D. R. METTEE and E. ARONSON, "Affective Reactions to Appraisal From Others," in T. L. Huston (Ed.), *Foundations of Interpersonal Attraction* (New York: Academic Press, 1974), pp. 235–283. I highly recommend this article to the reader who is interested in studying research on personal evaluations in more detail.

4 P. SKOLNICK, "Reactions to Personal Evaluations: A Failure to Replicate," *Journal of Personality and Social Psychology*, 1971, 18, 62–67.

5 J. S. SHRAUGER and S. C. JONES, "Social Validation and Interpersonal Evaluations," *Journal of Experimental Social Psychology*, 1968, 4, 315–323.

6 L. JACOBS, E. BERSCHEID, and E. WALSTER, "Self-Esteem and Attraction," *Journal of Personality and Social Psychology*, 1971, 17, 84–91.

7 J. E. DITTES, "Attractiveness of Group as a Function of Self-Esteem and Acceptance by Group," *Journal of Abnormal and Social Psychology*, 1959, 59, 77–82.

8 C. W. BACKMAN and P. F. SECORD, "The Effect of Perceived Liking on Interpersonal Attraction," *Human Relations*, 1959, 12, 379–384.

9 S. C. JONES and D. PANITCH, "The Self-Fulfilling Prophecy and Interpersonal Attraction," *Journal of Experimental Social Psychology*, 1971, 7, 356–366.

10 E. ARONSON and P. WORCHEL, "Similarity vs. Liking as Determinants of Interpersonal Attractiveness," *Psychonomic Science*, 1966, 5, 157–158.

11 O. J. HARVEY and W. F. CLAPP, "Hope, Expectancy and Reactions to the Unexpected," *Journal of Personality and Social Psychology*, 1965, 2, 45–52.

12 S. C. JONES and D. J. SCHNEIDER, "Certainty of Self-Appraisal and Reactions to Evaluations From Others," *Sociometry*, 1968, 31, 395–403.

13 D. R. METTEE and E. ARONSON, "Affective Reactions to Appraisal From Others."

14 D. CARNEGIE, *op. cit.*, p. 39.

15 M. DEUTSCH and L. SOLOMON, "Reactions to Evaluation by Others as Influenced by Self-Evaluation," *Sociometry*, 1959, 22, 93–112.

16 R. C. HOWARD and L. BERKOWITZ, "Reactions to the Evaluators of One's Performance," *Journal of Personality*, 1958, 26, 496–506.

17 D. G. DUTTON and A. J. ARROWOOD, "Situational Factors in Evaluation Congruency and Interpersonal Attraction," *Journal of Personality and Social Psychology*, 1971, 18, 222–229.

18 D. LANDY and E. ARONSON, "Liking for an Evaluator as a Function of His Discernment," *Journal of Personality and Social Psychology*, 1968, 9, 133–141.

19 H. DICKOFF, "Reactions to Evaluations by Another Person as a Function of

Self-Evaluation and the Interaction Context," Unpublished doctoral dissertation, Duke University, 1961. Cited in E. E. Jones, *op. cit.*, pp. 169–178.

20 C. A. LOWE and J. W. GOLDSTEIN, "Reciprocal Liking and Attributions of Ability: Mediating Effects of Perceived Intent and Personal Involvement," *Journal of Personality and Social Psychology*, 1970, 16, 291–297.

21 A. PEPITONE and J. SHERBERG, "Intentionality, Responsibility and Interpersonal Attraction," *Journal of Personality*, 1957, 25, 757–766.

22 E. WALSTER and L. FESTINGER, "The Effectiveness of 'Overheard' Persuasive Communications," *Journal of Abnormal and Social Psychology*, 1962, 65, 395–402.

23 E. E. JONES, *op. cit.*, p. 30.

24 E. ARONSON and D. LINDER, "Gain and Loss of Esteem as Determinants of Interpersonal Attractiveness," *Journal of Experimental Social Psychology*, 1965, 1, 156–172.

25 This issue is discussed by E. Aronson and D. Linder and by D. R. Mettee and E. Aronson.

26 H. W. STEVENSON, R. KEEN, and R. M. KNIGHTS, "Parents and Strangers as Reinforcing Agents for Children's Performance," *Journal of Abnormal and Social Psychology*, 1963, 183–186.

27 H. B. GERARD and C. W. GREENBAUM, "Attitudes Toward an Agent of Uncertainty Reduction," *Journal of Personality*, 1962, 30, 485–495.

28 J. C. STAPERT and G. L. CLORE, "Attraction and Disagreement-Produced Arousal," *Journal of Personality and Social Psychology*, 1969, 13, 64–69.

29 XENOPHON, *Memorabilia* (London: Heinemann, 1923), p. 48. Cited in E. Walster, G. W. Walster, J. Piliavin, and L. Schmidt, "Playing 'Hard-to-Get': Understanding an Elusive Phenomenon," *Journal of Personality and Social Psychology*, 1973, 26, 113–121.

30 OVID, *The Art of Love* (Bloomington: University of Indiana Press, 1963), pp. 65–66. Cited in E. Walster, G. W. Walster, J. Piliavin, and L. Schmidt, *op. cit.*

31 E. WALSTER, G. W. WALSTER, J. PILIAVIN, and L. SCHMIDT, *op. cit.*

32 E. E. JONES, *op. cit.*, pp. 38–39.

33 G. L. CLORE and B. BALDRIDGE, "Interpersonal Attraction: The Role of Agreement and Topic Interest," *Journal of Personality and Social Psychology*, 1968, 9, 340–346.

34 J. LOMBARDO, R. WEISS, and W. BUCHANON, "Reinforcing and Attracting Functions of Yielding," *Journal of Personality and Social Psychology*, 1972, 21, 359–368.

35 E. E. JONES, K. J. GERGEN, and K. E. DAVIS, "Some Determinants of Reactions to Being Approved or Disapproved as a Person," *Psychological Monographs*, 1962, 76, Whole No. 521.

36 P. M. BLAU, "A Theory of Social Integration," *American Journal of Sociology*, 1960, 65, 545–557.

37 E. E. JONES, K. J. GERGEN, and R. G. JONES, "Tactics of Ingratiation Among Leaders and Subordinates in a Status Hierarchy," *Psychological Monographs*, 1963, 77, Whole No. 566.

38 E. ARONSON, B. WILLERMAN, and J. FLOYD, "The Effect of a Pratfall on Increasing Interpersonal Attractiveness," *Psychonomic Science*, 1966, 4, 227-228.

39 R. HELMREICH, E. ARONSON, and J. LEFAN, "To Err is Humanizing—Sometimes: Effects of Self-Esteem, Competence, and a Pratfall on Interpersonal Attraction," *Journal of Personality and Social Psychology*, 1970, 16, 259-264.

40 M. WIENER and A. MEHRABIAN, *Language Within Language: Immediacy, a Channel in Verbal Communication* (New York: Appleton-Century-Crofts, 1968).

41 B. KAPLAN, "An Experimental Study of the Relation of Formal Aspects of Speech Behavior to Role-Taking Activity," Unpublished doctoral dissertation, Clark University, 1953. Cited in M. Wiener and A. Mehrabian, *op. cit.*, pp. 111-112.

42 A. MEHRABIAN and M. WIENER, "Non-Immediacy Between Communicator and Object of Communication in a Verbal Message: Application to the Inference of Attitudes," *Journal of Consulting Psychology*, 1966, 30, 420-425.

43 R. GOTTLIEB, M. WIENER, and A. MEHRABIAN, "Immediacy, DRQ, and Content in Verbalizations About Positive and Negative Experiences," *Journal of Personality and Social Psychology*, 1967, 7, 266-274.

44 A. MEHRABIAN and M. WIENER, "Non-Immediacy Between Communicator and Object of Communication in a Verbal Message: Application to the Inference of Attitudes."

45 A. MEHRABIAN, "Differences in the Forms of Verbal Communication as a Function of Positive and Negative Affective Experience," Unpublished doctoral dissertation, Clark University, 1964. Cited in M. Wiener and A. Mehrabian, *op. cit.*, p. 116.

46 A. MEHRABIAN, "Attitudes in Relation to the Forms of Communicator-Object Relationship in Spoken Communications," *Journal of Personality*, 1966, 34, 80-93.

47 A. MEHRABIAN, "Attitudes Inferred From Non-Immediacy of Verbal Communications," *Journal of Verbal Learning and Verbal Behavior*, 1967, 6, 294-295.

48 A. MEHRABIAN, "Communication Length as an Index of Communicator Attitude," *Psychological Reports*, 1965, 17, 519-522.

49 A. MEHRABIAN, "Immediacy: An Indicator of Attitudes in Linguistic Communication," *Journal of Personality*, 1966, 34, 26-34.

50 A. MEHRABIAN, "Attitudes Inferred From Neutral Verbal Communications," *Journal of Consulting Psychology*, 1967, 31, 414-417.

51 C. L. KLEINKE, R. A. STANESKI, and P. WEAVER, "Evaluation of a Person Who Uses Another's Name in Ingratiating and Noningratiating Situations," *Journal of Experimental Social Psychology*, 1972, 8, 457-466.

52 R. A. STANESKI, C. L. KLEINKE, and F. B. MEEKER, "Effects of Ingratiation, Touch, and Use of Name on Evaluation of Job Applicants and Interviewers," Paper presented at the meeting of the Western Psychological Association, Anaheim, Calif., 1973.

53 C. L. KLEINKE, R. A. STANESKI, and P. WEAVER, *op. cit.*

54 *Ibid.*

55 C. L. Kleinke, F. B. Meeker, and C. La Fong, "Effects of Gaze, Touch and Use of Name on Evaluation of 'Engaged' Couples," *Journal of Research in Personality*, 1974, 7, 368–373.

56 P. C. Cozby, "Self-Disclosure, Reciprocity and Liking," *Sociometry*, 1972, 35, 151–160.

57 M. Worthy, A. L. Gary, and G. M. Kahn, "Self-Disclosure as an Exchange Process," *Journal of Personality and Social Psychology*, 1969, 13, 59–63.

58 B. C. Certner, "Exchange of Self-Disclosures in Same-Sexed Groups of Strangers," *Journal of Consulting and Clinical Psychology*, 1973, 40, 292–297.

59 V. J. Derlega, M. S. Harris, and A. L. Chaikin, "Self-Disclosure Reciprocity, Liking and the Deviant," *Journal of Experimental Social Psychology*, 1973, 9, 277–284.

60 P. C. Cozby, "Self-Disclosure: A Literature Review," *Psychological Bulletin*, 1973, 79, 73–91.

61 Z. Rubin, *Liking and Loving* (New York: Holt, Rinehart and Winston, 1973), pp. 162–168.

62 D. Carnegie, *op. cit.*, p. 93.

63 *Ibid.*, p. 109.

Subject Index

Name Index